balanced
brand

balanced
brand

HOW TO BALANCE
THE STAKEHOLDER FORCES
THAT CAN MAKE OR BREAK YOUR BUSINESS

JOHN FOLEY

WITH JULIE KENDRICK

JOSSEY-BASS
A Wiley Imprint
www.josseybass.com

Published by Jossey-Bass
A Wiley Imprint
989 Market Street, San Francisco, CA 94103-1741   www.josseybass.com

Readers should be aware that Internet Web sites offered as citations and/or sources for further information may have changed or disappeared between the time this was written and when it is read.

Jossey-Bass books and products are available through most bookstores. To contact Jossey-Bass directly call our Customer Care Department within the U.S. at 800-956-7739, outside the U.S. at 317-572-3986, or fax 317-572-4002.

Jossey-Bass also publishes its books in a variety of electronic formats. Some content that appears in print may not be available in electronic books.

Library of Congress Cataloging-in-Publication Data
Foley, John, 1955-
    Balanced brand : how to balance the stakeholder forces that can make
or break your business / by John Foley with Julie Kendrick.-1st ed.
       p. cm.
    Includes bibliographical references (p.   ) and index.
    ISBN-13: 978-0-7879-8309-3 (cloth)
    ISBN-10: 0-7879-8309-8 (cloth)
    1. Brand name products. 2. Corporate image. 3. Relationship marketing.
4. Product management.   I. Kendrick, Julie. II. Title.
HD69.B7.F65 2006
658.8'27-dc22
                                            2005034283

Printed in the United States of America
FIRST EDITION
HB Printing   10 9 8 7 6 5 4 3 2 1

Contents

To
Joe Foley, who taught me values for living,
and
Burt Cohen, who taught me values for business

More than 62 million people witnessed a political debate . . . the same stimulus, at the same time. Amazingly, half the country selectively heard one message, while the other half heard something completely different.

What made the difference were the personal values people used to filter and interpret what they saw and heard.

Values are what drive behavior in politics, commerce, and your business.

Companies that do the best job aligning their corporate values with key stakeholder values will rule the marketplace.

Preface

Sustained corporate growth and profitability are predicated on having strong, long-term relationships. Without common values there are no relationships. Without relationships there is no business.

Values and corporate cultures are often seen as the "soft side" of business. Conventional business wisdom dictates that free markets, quarterly financials, and stock performance are the "real stuff" of business. Today's CEOs are given, on average, only three to five years to prove their worth, based on making their numbers each quarter. Employees are treated as a line item liability on the balance sheet. The problem with this thinking is that it puts numbers before people. While analysts and investors focus on the numbers, without loyal customers, talented leadership, and dedicated work staff, there would be no numbers. Great companies that have successfully built long-term equity share an enlightened view of the importance of building a consistent set of operating values and a strong corporate culture.

Customers, employees, shareholders, and anyone else who plays a role in the success of your company are your stakeholders. Every stakeholder applies their personal and professional values to judge the performance of your company, which is reflected in the strength of your brand and reputation. When your corporate values are out of alignment with your stakeholders' values, trouble is right around the corner.

When Nike sourced Third World labor to help the bottom line, they never considered that customers would care about manufacturing processes.

The Wal-Mart senior executives who aggressively managed labor costs in the pursuit of lower retail prices and higher profit margins never gained the input and support from employees.

What you don't know *can* hurt you, especially in today's volatile business environment. Stakeholder values dictate behavior in the free market system. Earnings, profit, and loss are the by-products of market behavior, but stakeholder values are the forces behind building or destroying brands and reputations. Surprisingly, many of these values are rarely measured, because customers assign their personal values to a brand *after* the purchase. Employee, vendor, shareholder, and community values can go unnoticed until a company does something that violates personal or business standards, causing loss of sales, public backlash, and lawsuits.

The BalancedBrand approach is the assessment and alignment of your company's values with key stakeholders' values. Without clearly understanding what's important to all the people your business touches, it's impossible to create a strong brand and reputation in the marketplace, and the vision of your company will fall short without continuous internal and external alignment.

In this book we show you how to use the Balanced Brand principles to gain the insights and tools you need to continually assess stakeholder values that create a powerful alignment between your organization and your stakeholders. BalancedBrand puts you in control of building and protecting your brand and reputation.

The Story Behind *BalancedBrand*

As founder and owner of a brand agency, I've had the opportunity to do brand work with more than 120 companies since 1986. Our sole focus had always been on helping our clients influence purchasing behavior. We identified the customer insights that drive sales while making the most compelling arguments for our clients' products and services, which is the traditional work of marketers.

Three years ago I had an experience that dramatically changed the way I thought about marketing. While traveling in northern Thailand, I happened to visit a silk factory that specialized in hand-woven scarves. The scarves were exquisite, and the craftsmanship was outstanding. Best of all, they were priced at about $5 U.S. The manager asked if we'd like to see how the scarves were made. We were delighted to learn more.

He brought us into the back, where approximately fifty women were using antiquated looms to weave the scarves. The conditions were sweltering, and it was questionable from the scarves' low retail prices whether these women could earn a livable wage.

I was instantly conflicted. On the one hand, I really loved the workmanship and products, but I felt I would be exploiting these workers. It was against my personal value system to take advantage of other people. Ultimately, we did make a purchase, but the whole experience made me feel guilty.

Later that night, I woke up and started to think about how communications, and specifically the Internet, influence people's attitudes and behaviors based on their values. It occurred to me that all generations younger than the Baby Boomers have grown up being globally connected on the Internet and thereby understand that purchasing decisions they make directly affect jobs and working conditions around the world. This experience became the impetus for evaluating numerous companies and industries in order to better understand how values alignment affected stakeholder behavior, corporate cultures, brands, reputations, and ultimately market performance.

Given the publicity around the Nike sweatshop story, you'd say we should already know that. However, business spends the lion's share of its money and resources to determine why people buy a product or service—but puts little or no resources toward understanding their customers' values *after* the purchase. For many customers, the relationship with the company or brand begins once they've made a decision to purchase, because they now see the brand as a reflection of their judgment and values. Even less money is spent on understanding employee, shareholder, vendor, and community values. People assign their values to a brand or company without the company's knowledge. It's only after a major market shift or crisis that companies discover the extent to which they were rewarded or punished based on their ability to align with stakeholder values.

That's why every time you hear about backlash in the media, the company is always caught off guard. Companies, brands, and reputations are destroyed by not understanding these crucial hidden values. Because of corporate silos, CEOs shoulder the burden of managing all stakeholder groups—not just customers and shareholders. Appeasing their expectations has become one of the great challenges for CEOs in business. What's disconcerting is that when you ask senior managers who are their most influential stakeholders, the answer is usually the customer or the shareholder, without proper consideration for all the other groups who have direct impact on the company's success. So not only are companies falling short on knowing who their key stakeholders are, they have no tools to assess stakeholder values.

BalancedBrand delivers the systems and tools to assess and align corporate values with stakeholder values. Companies now have a new way to manage stakeholders that results in building and protecting a strong brand and a strong reputation.

The competitive advantages created by *BalancedBrand* can help any size company succeed. As long as advertising and public relations agencies continue to rely on outdated metrics rather than stakeholder values, the industry will continue to be ineffective and inconsistent in delivering strong brands and strong reputations.

The Challenge

As part of our research for this book, we heard from senior managers who struggle with the forces that bear down on their businesses with increasing pressure. They are facing unprecedented business challenges from foreign competition, outsourcing and the relentless cycle of reducing costs while adding value to compete in a global market. We heard about investors' and analysts' demands to meet quarterly performance expectations or face the wrath of Wall Street. Senior managers are also faced with unprecedented board of directors involvement and government regulation, as well as consumer and employee activism that has made business management extremely volatile. So many business decisions are now driven by the unsettling trend of customers who are slow to trust but quick to switch brands when they aren't completely satisfied.

Executives struggle with how they can consistently make the right decisions to "stay competitive" while avoiding the kind of backlash leveled at Nike, Wal-Mart, Microsoft, and countless other companies. Given the complexity of running a business with multiple stakeholders who have conflicting sets of values, it's no wonder that a company's vision and values can get trampled.

There Is a Way

The answer to this quandary lies in formally prioritizing your stakeholder groups. Not all stakeholders play an equal role in your company's success. It is imperative to understand where their values are in conflict with each other as well as with your organization. With this information, you can measure, analyze, and calibrate your business actions to align with the values of your most important stakeholders.

Businesses who haven't accurately assessed the power of their stakeholders' values risk being blindsided. The forces of stakeholder values exist and will impact your company's performance, regardless of whether or not you measure and act on their influences. The question is, Can you afford to ignore these critical business drivers? BalancedBrand helps you ask the right questions and ensure that you're consistently getting the answers you need to effectively respond to changing business conditions and take advantage of the dynamics in the marketplace. You will gain the ability to continually assess and align with evolving stakeholder values, which is the key to building and protecting your brand and reputation.

BalancedBrand delivers the insights to assess and align corporate values with key stakeholder groups. These shared values are the foundation to create long-term relationships. We've written this book for everyone who is involved in managing stakeholders, building loyalty, or creating and protecting strong brands and reputations: C-level executives, public affairs directors, brand managers, and anyone else with stakeholder responsibility.

We identify proven strategies that any size company can tap into to assess and align corporate actions and values with key stakeholders. It covers real-world ideas for helping you identify common ground to strengthen relationships with all constituencies, and it delivers a clear picture on how to prosper, no matter how hard market forces are trying to knock your company's brand and reputation off balance.

By implementing the principles of Balanced Brand in your business, you can be assured of achieving three of the most important factors in achieving your company's long-term success:

1. Optimize stakeholder relationships

2. Maximize brand strength

3. Foster a highly regarded reputation

With these three things accomplished, your company will realize increased sales, loyalty, and satisfaction.

This book is broken into two parts, Stakeholder Value Assessment and Stakeholder Values Alignment. Once your company masters these two concepts, creating and protecting a strong brand and a strong reputation will be yours to leverage in the marketplace.

Our goal is larger than simply publishing a business book. Our hope is that BalancedBrand will help you understand how values directly impact quality, service, jobs, the environment, and communities as well as your bottom line. The "values revolution" is a new movement that will change the way successful companies do business.

BalancedBrand is a process that works, and we hope you will put it to work for your company's future.

Minneapolis, Minnesota   John Foley
November 2005   Julie Kendrick

balanced
brand

Strong Brand, Strong Reputation

One Without the Other Creates Imbalance

The free market system is pure oxygen . . . the life-sustaining force in business.

——————

Greed, arrogance, and ambition ignite the destructive behavior in business.

——————

When sparks collide with pure oxygen, there's an explosion and everyone gets hurt.

——————

Only clear values and a strong corporate culture can create a true firewall between free markets and destructive behavior.

In traditional marketing, reputation is simply a dimension of brand. BalancedBrand brings the perspective that brand and reputation are really two sides of the same coin—and represent your complete business. Executives and marketers must understand that while brand and reputation are interdependent, they are not interchangeable. In fact, a brand is a set of promises, associations, images, and emotions that companies create to build loyalty with their customers. Brand is from the inside out. Your company controls your brand promise, position, and attributes.

Reputation, on the other hand, is outside in. A reputation is built on direct experiences, others' opinions, rumors, and third party validation from outside stakeholders and is shaped and formed by your company's and employees' actions, perceptions of your industry, origin, and stakeholder biases. Through BalancedBrand, the ultimate goal is to create and protect both a strong brand and a strong reputation.

[
Brand is inside out.

Reputation is outside in.
]

Brand and Reputation

A strong brand is a core element of a BalancedBrand, but it's just the start. Many top executives confuse having a strong brand with having an equally strong reputation. Because their product or service sells well, they presume their customers must love and respect them. After all, the proof is in the revenue numbers. This delusional thinking combined with hubris has led to catastrophes such as those of Arthur Andersen, WorldCom, and Enron.

[
A strong brand is only the start of a
BalancedBrand. Without the support provided
by a strong reputation, it can topple easily.
]

Occasionally, a formerly respected company gets saddled with arrogant or greedy leadership, and, along with SEC hearings, perp walks, and courtroom trials, brands that were once trusted and esteemed fail and die. These failures always involve carelessness with the organization's most precious asset, its reputation.

Immutable Laws

In his book *The 18 Immutable Laws of Corporate Reputation*, Ronald J. Alsop presents the value of establishing, keeping, and repairing reputations.[1] Alsop is a news editor and senior writer at the *Wall Street Journal* with expertise in covering corporate brands and reputations. His book explores how companies such as FedEx, Disney, GE, and The Home Depot have built or destroyed their reputations. What makes his book so relevant is the wide variety of industries covered from a journalistic point of view. Alsop does a terrific job of blending clear, concise stories with a step-by-step practical guide for building and protecting reputations.

Shifting Brands and Reputations

Brands and reputation shift from strong to weak depending on a company's action and changes in the marketplace. It is easy to believe that these shifts don't exist, because the changes in reputation are often subtle and occur over a long period of time. Occasionally, a major event or disaster erodes a brand or reputation overnight.

Brands can be affected by competition or abrupt changes in customer preference that erode brand strength quickly. The following matrix identifies how brands and reputations work in tandem.

Bulletproof brands and reputations—the ones that seem to grow and prosper year after year—are increasingly rare. There are many obstacles along the path to a strong brand and strong reputation, including market competition, shareholder demands, skyrocketing

Shifting Brands and Reputations

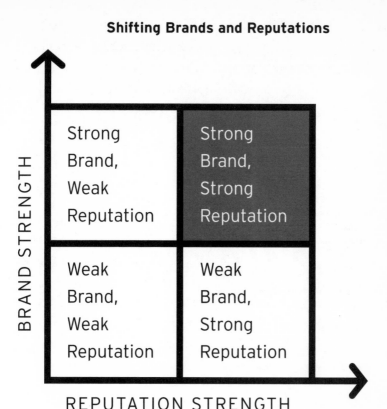

BRAND STRENGTH

Strong Brand, Weak Reputation	Strong Brand, Strong Reputation
Weak Brand, Weak Reputation	Weak Brand, Strong Reputation

REPUTATION STRENGTH

promotion costs, and the sheer velocity of innovation. Customers have also become so jaded that it's nearly impossible to build long-term trust and loyalty. Unfortunately, because Wall Street expects miracles every quarter, many companies feel that time is the one thing they can't spare. If an effort doesn't work overnight, it's quickly dumped in favor of the next "great idea." This continual churning of strategies is why so many companies have trouble executing a viable marketing plan. A lack of consistency is not only demoralizing to the whole organization but can destroy your brand and reputation. With an in-depth examination of brand and reputation strength, you'll see the interdependent relationships between brand and reputation and how they play out in the marketplace.

Strong Brand, Weak Reputation

More Is Falling Than the Prices

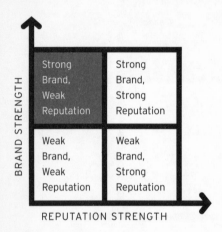

REPUTATION STRENGTH

When Sam Walton was alive, he understood that the essence of the Wal-Mart brand was sticking up for the little guy. Walton's positioning of Wal-Mart wasn't simply as a big discount store; it was an ally of its lower- and middle-class shoppers, working to get the best deals for the little guy. His homespun, friendly retailing style helped to turn Wal-Mart into the largest retailer in the world. More important, Walton also understood that the people who worked at Wal-Mart matched the demographics of his customer base.

Things have dramatically changed. Wal-Mart, being sued by its employees for exploitation, is facing the largest class action suit for sex discrimination in U.S. history.

The Associated Press reported that the company has aggressively fought employees' efforts to unionize. The company has also been criticized by the United Food and Commercial Workers union, which continues to try to organize Wal-Mart workers. Wal-Mart is also struggling with community backlash.

Most prominent was the failed attempt in 2004 to put a store in Inglewood, California, where the retailer lost a referendum that painted the company as an unwanted source of traffic and low-paying jobs.

In response to reported criticisms, Wal-Mart's chief executive Lee Scott went on the offense. On January 12, 2005, the company took out more than 100 full-page newspaper ads outlining the wages and benefits it pays its employees and the good the Bentonville-based company says it brings to communities.

The ad states that the company's average pay is nearly twice the minimum wage, that 74% of its hourly workers are full time, and that Wal-Mart offers health and life insurance, company stock, and a 401(k) retirement plan. Wal-Mart has more than 1 million domestic employees.

Scott said he wants Wal-Mart to overcome its reputation as a company that does not pay well and has minimal full-time workers. "We're taking this time to say, 'Hold on a minute, we have good jobs,'" Scott said.[2] "I thought it was ridiculous," Scott said of the attention drawn by the Inglewood failure. "We had a record number of stores open this past year . . . [and] this year we will open a record number of stores." Scott said no one source of criticism prompted the new offensive. "I liken it to being nibbled to death by guppies," Scott said.

Mr. Scott may discover the guppies are sharks.

Wal-Mart risks eroding its market position because it seems to lack an understanding of the customer, employee, community, and vendor values that drive relationships and loyalty. Thus far Wal-Mart's efforts to address these issues have resulted in ambivalence in the marketplace. There isn't a clear opinion on Wal-Mart's reputation.

The business question is, how will Wal-Mart's labor practices impact its reputation and sales in the long term?

If you put aside your personal values or business ethics and look strictly from a revenue perspective, the question becomes, Is it cheaper to pay more for labor in order to protect Wal-Mart's reputation? All of the millions of dollars that Wal-Mart has invested in building its brand as "the place with friendly employees and falling prices" are at risk because of weak reputation.

While Wal-Mart has built its business on low-cost labor, economies of scale, total supply chain management, and the best inventory system in retail, their operational excellence has only managed an average net profit margin of 3.4% for the past five years. In contrast, Target has built its business model around values alignment with its customers. Target has built its business model on superior merchandising to customers' desire for design, contemporary shopping experience, and low cost. Target's average net profit margin is 4.3% for the past five years. Target has built a clear brand and reputation advantage over Wal-Mart.

The question remains, how many weak relationships can any company afford to have regardless of size? At last count, Wal-Mart has strained relationships with many of its vendors, employees, and communities. Wal-Mart will be a pivotal test case for the importance of stakeholder values alignment.

[Weak relationships offset the strength
of healthy brands.]

Weak Brand, Strong Reputation

Fender Takes Its Licks

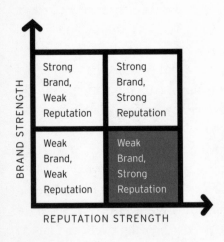

In 1948, Leo Fender revolutionized the electric guitar industry by introducing the Fender Broadcaster, which was quickly renamed the legendary Fender Telecaster. The Fender Stratocaster, launched in 1954, was arguably the most popular guitar ever made. These guitars offered a unique sound that is still sought by rock-and-roll stars like Eric Clapton. Fender guitar aficionados will tell you that if you want a real Fender, you have to buy one made between 1948 and 1965. That's because after serious illness in 1965, Leo Fender sold his company to CBS and, in the opinion of experts, ruined the quality of the guitars. Today you can buy an old Fender for up to $10,000 or a new Fender for around $300. The Fender reputation has still been able to sustain a weak brand because of its product history, not its cheap, imported knockoffs.

The Brand Has No Teeth

While reputation is enough to carry some companies, the National Hockey League (NHL) is facing a very different problem. The NHL has a very loyal fan base and has traditionally enjoyed a very strong reputation among those followers. The recent player lockout and lost season may have severely damaged the NHL's biggest asset, its reputation. That threat put the league in extreme peril because it falls significantly short in brand value delivery when compared with other professional sports. The league has never been able to garner

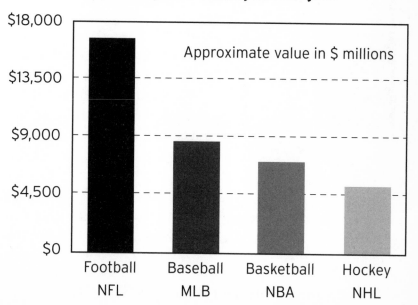

Big Four Sports: Valuing the Leagues

the television audience necessary to generate large revenues. The numbers tell the story: the National Football League (NFL) has nearly $20 billion in deals from various networks. Major League Baseball has more than $3 billion, the National Basketball Association (NBA) has nearly $5 billion, and the NHL has only $600 million.[3]

And while its followers are loyal, hockey is not a sports brand that has caught on with the majority of Americans. According to this recent Harris Poll, pro football is by far the nation's favorite sport. Hockey was the favorite of only one-ninth as many fans as the NFL, ranking below baseball, the NBA, auto racing, college football and basketball. It's certainly no surprise that no matter how loyal the fans or how great the players, the brand value of the NHL is four times less than that of the NFL.

Weak Brand, Weak Reputation

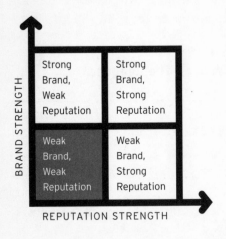

There are thousands of businesses you've never heard of in this category. They are not well known in the community nor do they have any kind of recognizable reputation. Each year many businesses fail because their customers, employees, and community are underwhelmed by mediocre products or services. Successful companies can also fall prey to Weak Brand and Weak Reputation.

Kmart, Squirt, Atari, Wang, and Oldsmobile are all examples of companies that have either gone out of business or are struggling to stay in business because they have Weak Brand and Weak Reputation.

Strong Brand, Strong Reputation

The Famous Blue Box

The most enviable position is to have a strong brand and a strong reputation, although few companies have been able to hold that position over the long term. Tiffany & Co. is one of the exceptions. Tiffany & Co. has been making heirlooms since 1837. With more than 7,000 employees and 100 stores worldwide, Tiffany & Co. has built earnings of more than

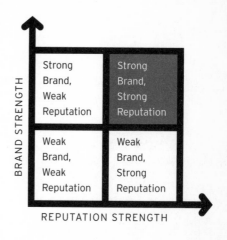

$300 million on sales of more than $2.2 billion in 2004. Though the company is working through a recent revenue decline, its long-term performance has been nothing short of spectacular. The distinctive blue box was introduced 138 years ago and continues to symbolize world-renowned quality and craftsmanship. Tiffany & Co. built its reputation on such icons as designing a presidential inauguration pitcher for President Lincoln, creating Union Army swords used by Generals Grant and Sherman, redesigning the Great Seal of the United States of America (still on the back of every $1 bill), introducing the famous Tiffany setting of a six-prong diamond solitaire engagement ring, and designing the Super Bowl trophy.

Since its inception, Tiffany & Co. has been the stuff of legends, including Truman Capote's 1958 classic *Breakfast at Tiffany's*. Not only has it built one of the strongest brands and reputations in the world, but Tiffany & Co. continues to find and cultivate new generations of clientele. In 1974, Elsa Perretti introduced her exclusive silver jewelry collection, which is wildly popular with 18- to 25-year-old women.

From a philanthropic perspective, Tiffany & Co. strengthens its reputation by contributing to and actively participating in local communities where the company does business. Through a culture of quality, service, and innovation, Tiffany & Co. is one of the best-known and most respected brands in the world.

Mining Values   Tiffany & Co. Chairman and CEO Michael Kowalski understands the importance of aligning Tiffany's values with its stakeholders.

In an open letter to Forest Service Chief Dale Bosworth, published March 23, 2004, in the *Washington Post,* Kowalski criticized the agency for approving the Rock Creek Mine.[4]

According to the *Spokesman-Review* in Idaho, the proposed mine would extract silver and copper by boring underneath the wilderness area in Montana, which is home to endangered grizzly bears and lynx. It would also discharge wastewater into a tributary of Lake Pend Oreille.

"We're certainly one of the world's largest consumers of diamonds, silver and platinum," Michael Kowalski acknowledged in a phone interview with the *Spokesman-Review.*

"But we've always believed that mine development should respect the environment," he said. "In this case, we believe that the recreation values represent a more valuable resource than the minerals."

Consumers want to buy jewelry with a good conscience, Kowalski said. Tiffany's—long associated with the very best in jewelry—promises that as part of its brand.

"There's an expectation . . . that the precious metals and gemstones crafted into our jewelry were produced in ways we all would be proud of," he said.[5]

Not all of Tiffany's stakeholders were in agreement with the company's position. Tiffany's statement on the Rock Creek Mine, however, shocked the mining industry. The project hadn't been in the national spotlight before. While permits were issued for the Rock Creek Mine, Kowalski's public position on environmental issues stirred a national debate.

On September 16, 2004, Jewelers of America, the industry trade group representing manufacturing and retail jewelers, announced a new set of standards for social responsibility. The standards reflected Tiffany & Co.'s position on silver mining.[6]

Only the Best   Being a world-renowned designer, craftsperson, or retail specialist is not enough to be able to work at Tiffany & Co. The indoctrination of all Tiffany employees is rigorous. Each employee is taught Tiffany's values for world-class quality, uncompromising service, and social responsibility. All associates are expected to be able to tie the famous Tiffany's bow that adorns every blue box. Jewelers working in the back room are expected to wear coat and tie as a reminder that they are the keepers of the Tiffany's tradition for making heirlooms for the next generation. Tiffany's focus on changing values has resulted in unprecedented success in their category. They lead their industry with an estimated 19% share of the $50,000 plus jewelry market.[7] Their net profit margin has averaged 11.7% over the past five years. Few other companies have been as consistent in living its values as Tiffany. This is the foundation of their greatness.

In the Interests of Patients

Health care is one of the most complex services to deliver. Unlike other businesses, health care delivery relies on a model of both for-profit and nonprofit. Few organizations have been able to bridge that gap as well as Mayo Clinic. The relevance of this example lies in how Mayo has used its values to overcome the complexity of healthcare. Mayo Clinic has been long recognized as one of the best private group practice, education, and research institutions in the world. Royalty, presidents, the rich and famous, along with another 500,000 people looking for a miracle or the best care available come to Mayo Clinic each year. What makes Mayo so special?

Mayo Clinic has been able to achieve and maintain world-class status through vigilant adherence to its principles and culture established back in 1910 by Doctors William and Charles Mayo. Ask anyone who works in Mayo Clinic what the key cultural value is, and they will tell you, "The needs of the patient come first." This is a distillation of the vision and values set by Dr. William Mayo. Dr. Mayo identified three principles that he felt were crucial to the future of Mayo Clinic:

1. Continuing pursuit of the ideal of service and not profit
2. Continuing primary and sincere concern for the care and welfare of each individual patient
3. Continuing interest by every member of the staff in the professional progress of every other member[8]

Using these guiding principles, the Mayo care model has built its renowned medical practice based on collaboration, the elimination of financial barriers, and an egalitarian physician and staff model that reinforces teamwork over individual accomplishments. Patients don't just get a doctor, they get Mayo Clinic. Using their collaborative culture, Mayo is able to tap into some of the world's most qualified medical experts and specialists to treat each unique medical challenge. Doctors at Mayo Clinic say, "When the going gets tough, I share my stuff." In other words, they work together to share resources and support each other to deliver exemplary service.

These principles are the foundation for the values and continuous success of Mayo Clinic. With more than 46,000 staff and physicians serving patients each year, Mayo Clinic's success is predicated on everyone sharing one set of values. As a result, Mayo

Clinic is able to provide the best care to every patient every day through integrated clinical practice, education, and research.

Word of Mouth   Mayo Clinic's strong brand and reputation was created through word of mouth. The majority of patients said good things about Mayo after their visits. In fact, 88% of all those who prefer Mayo reported that word of mouth from friends and family influenced their preference. Other significant sources included the media (62%) or a doctor's recommendation (56%).

To deliver the ideal service experience, the Mayo Clinic has developed a patient-centered Mayo Model of Service.

Dr. Leonard Berry, Distinguished Professor of Marketing in the May's School of Business at Texas A&M University, conducted an on-site study of Mayo Clinic's health care services and proclaimed, "Mayo Clinic leverages its core values as effectively as any organization we have ever studied." While studying Mayo Clinic's service, Dr. Berry found that the Mayo brothers' vision and values permeated the entire organization. During the annual weeklong "Heritage Days" celebration of Mayo Clinic, the famous Mayo brothers' quotations, especially those promoting the patient's interest first, appear in high-traffic spaces within the facilities. Mayo physicians are called "consultants" to reinforce the importance of conferring about their patients. Storytelling and repetition are vital for sustaining the values of Mayo's culture. States one longtime member of the staff, "I don't recall a speech or meeting I attended where the core values of the institution were not mentioned."

The cornerstone of Mayo Clinic's care model is the organization's ability to attract team players, according to Berry. Their entire recruiting process focuses on how well a candidate fits within the Mayo culture.[9] The investment in finding the right employees has resulted in remarkably low turnover rates. The national average turnover for nurses is 20%, whereas the turnover rate for Mayo hospital nurses in 2003 was 3%. Voluntary physician turnover rates at Mayo were less than 4%. It would be impossible to run an effective integrated, multi-disciplinary health care practice with high turnover rates.[10]

Mayo's commitment to teamwork, education, and research ensures that Mayo Clinic will remain in the forefront of medicine. Mayo Clinic is an extraordinary organization that has created a world-class brand and reputation by consistently living their values.

Management of brand and reputation strength is difficult without reliable measurement. In Chapter Two, we examine brand and reputation measurement models that will help you create a baseline for understanding your brand and reputation strength.

Chapter One Summary

Brand is inside out. Reputation is outside in.

Brand and reputation are not interchangeable.

Strong Brand, Strong Reputation

The goal of BalancedBrand is to have a strong brand and a strong reputation.

Measuring Brand and Reputation

Avoiding the Pitfalls That Can Destroy Your Brand and Reputation

In both brand and reputation you're only as strong as your ability to understand and align with key stakeholders.

Measuring Brand Strength

There are many ways of determining brand value—everything from building consumer value attitudinal models to determining net present value and future cash flows. And there has been increased demand to create a process that meets the needs of a diverse group of clients.

As one of the leading thinkers on this subject, Don Schultz, President of Agora, Inc., and Professor Emeritus-in-Service at Northwestern University, points out, "The limiting factor in most brand valuation approaches isn't the consumer focus." Indeed, the work of David Aaker, Kevin Lane Keller, Roland Rust, and a host of others have suggested that simply measuring consumer brand value is sufficient to understand and value a brand, because that's the area in which marketing operates.

In the more financially oriented approaches, organizations such as Interbrand, Future Brand, and BrandEconomics have focused on the net present value or estimated future cash flows the brand might generate. Inherently, these also focus on the actions of the brand's final customers and their actions in the marketplace, but assume that the income from the brand is more than just the value the customer places on the brand. However, the customer represents only one dimension of brand value.

Don Schultz has worked with the London-based brand consultancy, Brand Finance, to develop an innovative brand valuation framework. Unlike most financially based methodologies that focus primarily on future income flows from customers, their valuation and tracking model considers multiple groups that have either a direct or indirect impact on the organization and its success. Schultz believes that brand value measurement systems must include more than just the measures of the end user, because there are a host of other audiences and stakeholders that truly impact future shareholder value that can emanate from the brand. The model identifies six to eight or more key audiences that determine the current and future value of the brand.

"To really understand the true value and the complex dynamics that can influence the brand, one must understand how the various critical brand audiences value the brand as well as the final consumer. Although current practice does otherwise, looking only at the views, opinions, attitudes, and considerations of the end user, we have a limited perspective, that is, only a partial view of brand value," Schultz says.

The fundamentals of this model were developed in collaboration with David Haigh, Managing Director of Brand Finance, one of the leading British companies working on this subject. As Haigh says, "There is no longer room for 'black box' techniques that cannot be reconciled back to the management of the business." And,

A General Model for Brand Evaluation

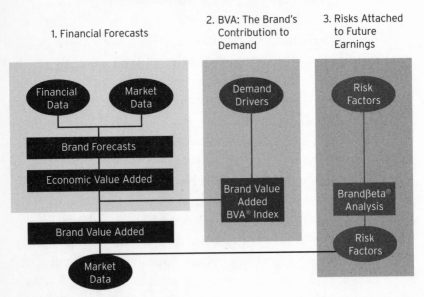

1. Financial Forecasts

2. BVA: The Brand's Contribution to Demand

3. Risks Attached to Future Earnings

Financial Data

Market Data

Brand Forecasts

Economic Value Added

Brand Value Added

Market Data

Demand Drivers

Brand Value Added BVA® Index

Risk Factors

Brandβeta® Analysis

Risk Factors

4. Valuation & Sensitivity Analysis

Source: Brand Finance plc

managers know that the end user, although an important ingredient in the mix, is only one part of the true value of the brand.

The model Schultz and Haigh have developed through Brand Finance is part of a three-step, highly transparent approach to brand valuation that is grounded in investment, business, and marketing theory. As Haigh points out, the valuation and scorecard methodology provides brand valuation solutions on a modular basis, fitting the approach to the particular client need. "That's totally unlike most other valuation models that force-fit the organization into an established approach or model," Haigh concluded.[1]

The Reputation Institute's Model for Reputation Measurement

The ultimate goal of a marketer is to create both a strong brand and a strong reputation. This combination is not only formidable in the marketplace, but is also financially rewarding. Charles Fombrun and Cees van Riel demonstrate the process through which reputations create wealth in their recent book, *Fame and Fortune*. The bottom-line effect occurs because reputations are an important contributor to consumers' purchase decisions.

As the authors suggest, however, "prevailing business logic insists on the exclusively rational and economic aspects of decision making."[2] According to Fombrun and van Riel, logical reasoning alone shortchanges the influence of perceptual and social factors on the decisions we make. In the decisions we make about what products to buy, we are heavily influenced not only by the objective features of those products, but by our *perceptions* of the companies that make them. That is, we are driven by our personal, emotional, and often irrational reactions to their offerings.

The Reputation Institute (RI), founded by Fombrun in 1997, has developed a standardized barometer called RepTrack® for measuring the reputations of companies, and regularly conducts surveys of the general public that evaluate some of the most visible companies in the world. RepTrack® asks people to describe their perceptions of a company on seven dimensions and twenty-two attributes. The key dimensions are defined as:

1. *Performance:* Perceptions of the company's financial results and prospects
2. *Workplace:* Perceptions of the company's workplace environment and the quality of its people
3. *Products:* Perceptions of the quality and price of the company's products and services
4. *Leadership:* Perceptions of how well the company is managed
5. *Citizenship:* Perceptions of the environmental strength and social responsibility of the company
6. *Governance:* Perceptions of the company's organizational systems and culture
7. *Innovation:* Perceptions of the company's entrepreneurial orientation and innovativeness

The RI's RepTrack® model is illustrated in the figure following. The Reputation Institute and its partners regularly track the reputations of the most visible companies in a wide range of countries, including the United States, South America, Europe, and Australia. Since 1999, the highest rated company in the U.S. studies has been the health care products company Johnson & Johnson. In France, the cosmetics company L'Oreal topped the ranking, as did carmaker Porsche in Germany, and Branson's Virgin Group in the United Kingdom. The results demonstrate considerable geographic diversity in the ratings that the public makes of companies. Perceptions of McDonald's, Microsoft, and The Coca-Cola Company, for instance, vary considerably across countries. These findings reinforce the

RepTrack®: The Reputation Institute's Reputation Measurement Model

© Reputation Institute

importance of carrying out customized analyses of reputation that examine not only the specific circumstances companies face in local markets, but dwell on the reasons why publics rate companies differently. Detailed statistical analysis typically demonstrates that the drivers of reputation also vary considerably among countries, with greater or lesser importance attributed to key dimensions such as citizenship and ethics. For instance, social factors like governance, citizenship, and ethics appear to have greater influence on public perceptions in countries that have been plagued by corporate scandals, particularly the United States and France.

The Reputations of the Most Visible Companies in 2004

United States		United Kingdom	
1. Johnson & Johnson	79.81	1. Virgin Group	77.2
2. 3M Company	79.07	2. Sony	76.1
3. The Coca-Cola Company	78.90	3. The Body Shop	74.4
4. The Procter & Gamble Company	78.26	4. Microsoft	74.1
5. United Parcel Service (UPS)	78.24	5. Tesco	72.8

Germany		France	
1. Porsche	75.4	1. L'Oreal	76.1
2. ALDI	75.2	2. Danone	73.5
3. BMW	73.2	3. Microsoft	69.8
4. Microsoft	70.0	4. PSA Peugeot Citroen	69.2
5. Siemens	69.0	5. Carefour	68.2

Reputation: Built in a Lifetime, Lost in a Moment

Apple's innovative. Microsoft's predatory. Volvos are safe.

Are these statements true? Our willingness to accept them is based on the source of the information. We are much more likely to believe what we read or hear from someone we trust. In our judicial system, you are innocent until proven guilty, but in the media, you are guilty until proven innocent. That's why it's important for your company to build strong and trusting relationships with the media. If the first time you ever talk to the media is when you're in trouble, you're in trouble. Media relations is different from crisis management. Having a solid media relations program is just part of becoming a recognized member of the community—and every single community that your brand reaches includes several media outlets that require relationship building.

Third Party Validation

The most candid comment people make about you may be said when you're not around. In the same way, the strongest part of your brand reputation comes from the comments and opinions of key stakeholders or industry experts.

It's not easy to get third party validation, but it can be done. There are a number of proven methods to build your company's reputation:

- Articulate your values to all constituencies.
- Align your corporate values with your key stakeholders' values.
- Empower employees and customers as ambassadors.
- Continually question how your products or services impact your stakeholders.
- Work within your industry to address problems and issues affecting the community or environment.
- Be active in the community.
- Give back.

Companies who employ these methods are recognized as industry leaders. Unfortunately, they are in the minority, because most companies are slow to realize the benefits of reputation building. Establishing a reputation as an industry leader takes a significant commitment of time and resources, with no guarantee of any short-term effect on the bottom line.

It's easy to understand why committing to reputation building feels like you can't afford the effort. The fact is, you can't afford not to. Your stakeholders will notice, for better or worse.

What's Your $640 Toilet Seat Story?

Every business has a "$640 Toilet Seat" story, a reference to the famous Pentagon overspending scandal of the 1980s. Obviously, the procurement pros at the Pentagon might have done well to ask vendors to sharpen their pencils on that toilet seat invoice. But many times, there are all sorts of reasons for any unusual line item or cost, and many possible explanations.

Imagine that when you get to work tomorrow, there's a gang of government auditors waiting for you. They announce, "We're here for the audit. Let's get started."

You begin to think about that last customer golf outing, or travel expense report, or presentation cost, or client gift. You wonder, can they all stand up under intense scrutiny? With a little effort, anyone can find a way to claim that you have mismanaged your company's money.

Expenditures and events taken out of context can easily look inappropriate when revealed in an audit or some other investigation. Consistent operating values increase the likelihood of the media or investigators giving you the benefit of the doubt. This is a common predicament for global companies doing business in countries where the standards for bribery and gift giving are different than in the United States. In these cases, it is imperative for organizations to operate with a single, consistent set of values regardless of potential lost opportunities. In the long run, your employees will appreciate not having to make the call when faced with an ethical dilemma.

Crisis Management

Many companies today rely on crisis management to ensure they have a plan when the unthinkable happens. Airlines, amusement parks, and food manufacturers have learned from experience that having an effective crisis management plan can mean the difference between success and disaster for their company. Even when a crisis occurs that is not the company's responsibility, the challenge is to mitigate the damage done from the first media cycle, which may be irreparable. Bad news always makes the front page, while exoneration is buried in the back of the paper. You may be right, but by the time the truth comes out, if it ever does, no one will know or care.

If you are wrong, the best response is to be forthcoming and apologize. And, the more quickly you admit fault and provide remedies, the more likely you are to save your brand and possibly your company's future.

Reputation and Mistakes

If you're thinking that companies with great reputations never make mistakes, you're wrong. Everyone makes mistakes, every day, sometimes before leaving the house in the morning or before responding to the first e-mail of the day. If you want to build a strong reputation, you need to accept that mistakes will happen and make a plan now about how to handle them. Here are some basic guidelines to follow when mistakes happen:

- Be honest.
- Take responsibility.
- Be willing to change and adapt.
- Be consistent.

How your entire organization responds under fire reflects the health of your corporate culture and values. The mark of all great companies is their ability to be resilient in the face of adversity.

Making a Mistake and Thriving: The Schwan Food Company

Schwan's is the largest direct-to-home food company in the United States, with multibillions in revenues and 700 national distribution depots. With 24,000 employees, they are the largest producer of frozen pizza and egg rolls in the country.

Here's an example of what happens when a company with strong corporate values is faced with a potential disaster. Their brand and reputation were severely challenged, but the steps they took to correct the problem may have strengthened their brand and reputation in the long run.

They might be the largest seller of frozen pizza and egg rolls, but Schwan's is most famous for ice cream, and that's where the trouble started. In 1994, more than 200,000 people were sickened in the largest single case of salmonella poisoning in the United States from a single food source—Schwan's ice cream.

The company didn't waste time assigning blame or denying that their product had caused the illness. They sent their home delivery truck drivers to every house on their routes, retrieved all the ice cream, then shut down production until the source of the problem was discovered and appropriate corrective action could be taken.

It turned out that an independent trucking contractor Schwan's used for hauling milk and ice cream had previously hauled raw eggs that were contaminated with *salmonella enteritis*. In the name of product safety and quality, Schwan's decided to cut out the middleman and bought their own fleet. And they didn't stop there. All dairy products used in making ice cream solutions are pasteurized twice—before and after transport.[3]

What has the impact been on Schwan's reputation? Customers appreciated the speed in addressing the problem and the way the company took responsibility for its actions—a typical customer response in describing the incident is that Schwan's "discovered they had a problem, they did the right thing."[4]

Without a clear set of corporate values, it is harder for anyone in the organization to consistently do the right thing. Acting on these values must start with top management and work its way into every level of the company. If people know what's expected of them, making the right call becomes easier, every time.

Redemption

One of the most difficult jobs is to repair a damaged brand or reputation. *Redemption* may seem like a theological term, but it also has a place in the business context.

If you were the general manager for Firestone, how would you make people believe that your tires are safe again? What happened when their Wilderness AT Tires led to rollovers on Ford Explorers was a tragedy for the victims, Firestone employees, and the community. This tragedy was such a serious breach of trust from a once-respected brand that it is doubtful that Firestone will ever recover. Firestone and Ford have ended their 100-year partnership, and redemption, in the eyes of many former customers, is very far away.

Redemption is much easier for rogue countries or religious scandals because they have time on their side. These institutions typically are around for many generations. Given enough time, redemption may be as simple as the institution outlasting the detractors. Most consumer brands could not survive one year, much less the three to five years it would take to begin rebuilding trust. Therefore redemption is not an option for most companies.

The Four Fatal Pitfalls of Brand Development

While having a strong brand and reputation creates the right environment for selling products and services, success is not guaranteed. It's not unusual for great companies to occasionally stumble in the marketplace. Having spent extensive money and resources on a new initiative, everyone believes the new effort will be a surefire winner. As soon as it becomes obvious that the initiative is a flop, the blame game begins. Upon closer examination, we find that these companies have committed one or more of the Four Fatal Pitfalls of Brand Development.

Pitfall Number 1: Weak Product or Service

Not all products or services are good. Some are ill conceived or don't deliver a relevant benefit to the customer. Instead of correcting the flawed product or improving service levels, some companies hold three-day off-site meetings where committees insist that poor marketing is the problem. The time-tested axiom still holds: Nothing can kill a bad product or service quicker than good marketing.

Pitfall Number 2: Poor Strategy

Building a strong brand and a strong reputation requires innovative, disciplined strategy. Some companies confuse a laundry list of selling tactics with strategic planning. A company's strategic planning flounders without clear values, positioning, and brand message.

Other companies rely on the same strategies regardless of changing market conditions, which parallels playing chess and making the same moves every game. How long do you think it would take the competition to beat you if they were paying attention? And some companies are so used to operating in "full panic mode," due to lack of any real strategic planning, that critical decisions are being made on the fly.

Pitfall Number 3: Lack of Research

Many companies believe that research is an expensive luxury they either don't require or can't afford. Having no research is like putting up a big wall on the playing field and only occasionally getting a glimpse of what's happening on the other side. You need research to help you check in with your stakeholders' attitudes and your competitors' actions.

Pitfall Number 4: Relying on Limited Marketing Tools

We once had a client who told us he didn't believe in advertising. We told him advertising is not a religion. You don't have to believe in it. But if it works, you had better use it. If you're not using all the tools available to you, and your competition is using them, you've

put yourself at a formidable disadvantage. Arguing whether advertising is more effective than public relations, or that direct mail is
more effective than Internet marketing, is like going to a hardware
store and arguing the merits of a hammer versus a saw. Without a
blueprint to work from (which is your strategic plan), none of the
tools are very effective at all.

The Secret Success Tool No One Can Wait For

Even if you have a strong product, solid strategy, credible research,
and the right mix of marketing tools, there's still one more element
in creating a strong brand and strong reputation. It's the one element very few people in our business are patient enough to wait for.

You need time.

[The secret ingredient for a strong brand
and reputation: Time.]

People have become increasingly more wary of business and
brands. We are not willing to trust or be loyal without a certain
amount of consistent and positive experience.

Unfortunately, many dot.com companies tried to build brands
at the speed of technology instead of the speed of humanity. We all
know the outcome. New products and services need time to cultivate relationships with an audience. The conundrum is knowing
when a product or service isn't filling a real need versus having the
patience to let the idea work.

Chapter Two Summary

Brand Strength
A method of evaluating a brand by measuring its financial strength, stakeholder support, and overall brand awareness.

Reputation Strength
The Reputation Institute has created a standardized research tool called RepTrack® which is designed to measure reputation strength. Reputation varies with culture and country and needs to be measured with global marketing in mind.

Third Party Validation
Third party validation is the essential source for building a reputation.

Crisis Management
Without an effective crisis management plan, your company will not be prepared when disaster strikes.

You can make a major corporate mistake and recover—follow The Schwan Food Company example.

Four Pitfalls of Brand Development

1. Weak product or service
2. Poor strategy
3. Lack of research
4. Relying on limited marketing tools

Secret Success Tool
The secret success tool no one can wait for: Time.

The BalancedBrand System

Taking Control of Your Brand and Reputation

Brands are the seeds of growth.

Values are the roots that grow deep.

Reputations are the bountiful harvest.

You reap what you sow.

[BalancedBrand: An essential business tool for creating and protecting strong brands and strong reputations. BalancedBrand continuously assesses and aligns corporate values with evolving stakeholder values.]

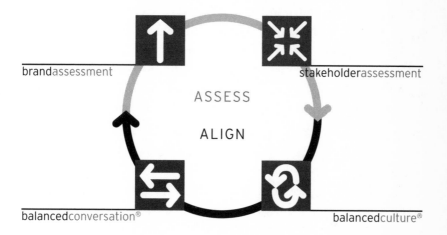

brandassessment   stakeholderassessment

ASSESS

ALIGN

balancedconversation®   balancedculture®

Many times, world events and market conditions are beyond our control. The BalancedBrand System is a way to reclaim control of *your world* by addressing the factors your organization can directly influence, such as customer loyalty, employee satisfaction, investor relations, and working with the community.

Although it's unrealistic to expect you can change your corporate values to align with your stakeholders' values overnight, creating alignment is the solution to many of your current problems. With The BalancedBrand System, many seemingly invisible factors driving your business begin to make a lot more sense.

Simply put, The BalancedBrand System gets you closer to your goals, however defined—category dominance, satisfied stockholders, or loyal customers. The BalancedBrand System provides the tools necessary to clearly prioritize stakeholders and assess stake-holder values. By understanding these values, you are able to define your brand, strengthen your reputation, and converse with your stakeholders in a new way.

Stakeholder values impact all areas of your business, not just marketing or public affairs. The sooner you start to think of your brand and reputation as a holistic business concept, the more easily you can use BalancedBrand to break down the communication and operating silos within your organization.

BalancedBrand creates stakeholder satisfaction by having the right manufacturing processes, service delivery, and employee dedication to building long-term relationships for your company. This is how great companies sustain market leadership, profitability, and growth. Your entire organization must get involved. With The BalancedBrand System, you can control many more factors than you ever thought possible.

In this chapter, we present a broad overview of The Balanced-Brand System. In the subsequent chapters, we examine each facet in greater detail.

Brand Assessment, Stakeholder Assessment

Brand Assessment

Brand Assessment is the internal foundation of The BalancedBrand System. By going through the exercise provided for identifying and validating corporate vision and values, you'll gain the insights necessary to understand how your organization aligns with outside stakeholder values. The crucial first step is to compare *Stated Values*, such as the written formal values found in annual reports or corporate literature, to *Operating Values*, the informal values employees use every day to run your business. Without internal alignment between stated and operating values, your organization will never achieve balance.

Next, you must complete the internal and external audit of your corporate brand and reputation strength to get a clear and accurate assessment of the current opinions held by key stakeholders.

Finally, Brand Assessment examines all aspects of your brand, including vision, values, brand, and reputation. Brand Assessment crosses the disciplines of sales, marketing, public relations, advertising, and interactive resulting in a holistic view of your organization. This information can be used as a platform for current marketing efforts as well as provide the reference source necessary for assessing your corporate values against stakeholder values.

Stakeholder Assessment

Stakeholder Assessment starts with the identification and prioritization of all stakeholder groups, such as customers, investors, employees, government, special interest groups, and the media. Not all stakeholder groups are equal. Clearly identifying your key stakeholders begins by pinpointing which groups have greatest impact on your business and future success. These key stakeholders determine which personal and professional values offer the greatest opportunity or threat to your organization.

The Stakeholder Assessment Pyramid is designed to assess and monitor a standardized set of three performance dimensions of stakeholder values:

1. *Aspiration:* Satisfying customers' needs and wants
2. *Process:* Understanding stakeholders' expectations of how a product is made or service is delivered
3. *Impact:* Understanding how stakeholders' values impact your product or service within the community or environment

Stakeholder Assessment Pyramid

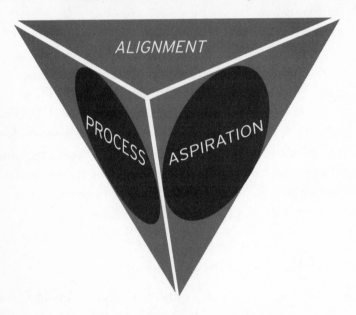

This group of standard values dimensions is further refined by using Stakeholder Values Maps. To locate potential opportunities and conflicts, this tool helps you compare and contrast the intensity of stakeholder values with your corporate values in the areas of Aspiration, Process, and Impact that represent potential opportunities and conflicts.

Every organization has its own unique set of shareholder values that must be monitored and measured. Without understanding all stakeholder values, most companies are in the dark about what's going on in their main constituents' heads and hearts. They are relying on hearsay and outdated experience to determine how their corporate actions impact long-term brand loyalty and reputation.

In the post-Enron era, public and media tolerance for corporate malfeasance is nonexistent. Companies that are slow to change find themselves sliding from being perennial media and Wall Street darlings to being attacked for poor business practices that were perfectly acceptable ten years ago. Most backlash is a result of companies having acted in ways that are out of balance with their stakeholders' values—values that continually evolve and change.

Ignorance of stakeholder values can be very dangerous for even the strongest brands. Customers, employees, stockholders, or special interest groups who become disillusioned by brand values that are out of line with their own values will discourage others from doing business with your company. If they get angry enough, a large-scale boycott or class action suit may be in the offing. Once the media jumps in, the company may be fighting to preserve its reputation and sometimes its survival. On the other hand, companies who are in balance with their stakeholders have a tremendous advantage over the competition in the marketplace.

In upcoming chapters, we further explore how stakeholders go about assigning values, and, even more important, how you can start to monitor the values that directly control your brand and reputation building.

Aligning Corporate and Stakeholder Values: Balanced Culture, Balanced Conversation

Balanced Culture

Without employee buy-in, your new initiative may become just another expensive advertising and public relations program with diminished results.

Changing corporate direction can pose a significant challenge for senior management. While it may be obvious that a major course adjustment is necessary, change is not possible without the entire organization working together. Within any company, there are those who resist change, those who eventually accept it, and those who are looking for constant change. With Balanced Culture, it becomes easier to identify the changes necessary to align corporate values with shareholder values.

Balanced Culture provides the communications framework through which the organization understands and appreciates the importance of alignment between corporate and stakeholder values. By creating a compelling narrative, organizations can achieve remarkable organizational changes that help employees understand and actively participate in a corporate vision of alignment.

Balanced Conversation

It's time to end the war! The war we continue to wage against our prospective customers, that is. Think of some of the words and phrases we use in our businesses: *Launch a campaign. Defend the position. Find the target. Capture the customer. Penetrate the market. Engage in a multilateral integrated advertising and public relations campaign.*

Customers aren't prisoners of war. They're people. And as people, they respond a lot better to conversations than to forced conversions. Simply bludgeoning your customers to death with repetitive advertising messages is like sitting next to the self-absorbed guy on the plane who Just. Won't. Stop. Talking. After a while, you tune him out and try to concentrate on the in-flight magazine to escape his diatribe. Customers do the same thing to you every day, only you can't hear them sigh or see them flip the pages or change channels.

Balanced Conversation is an innovative new method for creating authentic relationships and loyalty with each stakeholder group. The goal is to find common ground in telling your company's story, as well as relevant product and service stories, while continuously listening to your stakeholders' concerns.

It's not easy to create authentic brand-building conversations. You must be relentless in your willingness to initiate, sustain, and, when necessary, change the subject. Conversations are more difficult to execute than traditional marketing campaigns. However, the net result easily justifies the effort. If you want to jump ahead to learn more about stakeholder conversations, check out Chapter Seven, which covers that topic in depth.

Using The BalancedBrand System, you can help your organization identify the opportunities and competitive advantages of moving in a new direction. By focusing on and working closely with those who resist change, those who accept it, and those who seek constant change, your organization will be able to implement a balance more quickly and efficiently while ensuring that your goals don't get sidetracked.

By now, you know what basic steps you need to take in order to build and grow a strong brand and strong reputation. Without these skills, your company will always be susceptible to the shifting stakeholder values in the marketplace. The decision to be swept along with these powerful forces—or to control your destiny—is up to you.

Chapter Three Summary

BalancedBrand

An essential business tool for creating and protecting strong brands and strong reputations.

BalancedBrand continuously assesses and aligns corporate values with evolving stakeholder values.

The BalancedBrand System

The BalancedBrand System is comprised of:

The Assessment of Corporate and Stakeholder Values

- Brand Assessment
- Stakeholder Assessment

The Alignment of Corporate and Stakeholder Values

- Balanced Conversation
- Balanced Culture

Brand Assessment

Brand Assessment is a comprehensive overview of an organization's values, reputation, brand architecture, and position.

Stakeholder Assessment

The three dimensions of Stakeholder Assessment are Aspiration, Process, and Impact.

Stakeholder Values Maps measure the intensity of the values each group holds in the areas of Aspiration, Process, and Impact.

Balanced Culture

Organizational change to create alignment between your company and stakeholders can't happen without support at every level of the organization, from the top down.

Balanced Conversation

Conversations are more effective at building relationships than relying on repetitive messaging used in traditional advertising and public relations campaigns.

Using all stakeholder points of contact, it is possible to find innovative ways of delivering the creative content necessary to initiate and sustain conversations.

part one

Assessment of Organization and Stakeholder Values

Brand Assessment

brandassessment

What Shape Are Your Brand and Reputation In?

Carefully crafted images are designed to shape opinions . . . images of a company performing at its very best.

Acting according to one set of values is the only true test of long-term performance.

> [Brand Assessment is a comprehensive overview of an organization's values, reputation, brand, and position.]

Brand Assessment

Brand Assessment is a careful examination of your current vision, values, reputation, brand, and position. The process of executing Brand Assessment helps organizations compile this information into one accessible booklet that can be used by the entire organization.

There are excellent reference books that teach brand architecture for companies needing to do fundamental brand work. Two good primers are *United We Brand* by Mike Moser[1] and David A. Aaker's *Building Strong Brands.*[2]

Brand Assessment is the foundation of The BalancedBrand System. While most traditional brand models are designed to identify brand architecture, The BalancedBrand System is designed to help your company *apply* the principles for brand and reputation in a dynamic marketplace.

Vision

All successful companies begin with a clear, actionable vision. This premise explains why you are in business. A vision also explains where you are going. Without a vision most businesses flounder. Having a clearly defined vision is the wellspring of your whole organization. All processes and values are shaped around the vision. If you don't have one, or if it is the least bit ambiguous, crafting a cogent vision is imperative.

Corporate Values: Doing the Right Thing

Despite negative newspaper coverage, most companies try very hard to do the right thing in dealings with their employees, customers, and community. At the same time, determining "the right thing" can be difficult without a clear vision and values. If it's good for the shareholders at the expense of employees, is it right? What about if it's great for the company but detrimental to the environment?

Stated Values Versus Operating Values

A clear corporate vision surrounded by a set of well-articulated corporate values can help guide the way when the road gets rocky. More than just an exercise in business ethics, corporate values provide the blueprint for running your entire business. When carefully crafted and communicated properly, they help everyone in your organization understand the framework of what to do, how to do it, and why clear values are so important. Forget the glossy, nicely framed messages in the corporate lobby or in the annual report. These are *Stated Values*. Whenever you start a new job, someone takes you aside and says, "Let me tell you how things really work around here." These are *Operating Values*. In a perfect world, Stated Values and Operating Values are the same. However, it is imperative that you know the Operating Values of your organization because these are the values your stakeholders experience when dealing with your company. To build a clear set of Operating Values, you must identify what your organization stands for and what the people who work for you *believe* your company stands for.

When defining corporate values, simpler is always better. Your organization might value such things as:

- Treating people fairly
- Giving back to the community
- Being honest
- Striving for excellence
- Hiring talented people who are fun to work with
- Being stable and profitable

When you've identified the values that are critical to your organization, you've created the Operating Values on which to build your corporate reputation.

Corporate Reputation

All reputations are built over time, more through actions than through words. Our perceptions of reputations are created through personal interactions or the opinions of others. Your first step is to decide what key values you want stakeholders to know about your organization, such as:

- Great service
- Quality
- Reliability
- Trustworthiness
- Innovation

The conundrum is that consistency builds reputations, but people and organizations tend to be inconsistent. This may be because outside influences, such as unfounded rumors or existing opinions about your industry, are beyond your control. It may be because people in your organization don't follow or believe in your stated corporate values. No matter the inconsistencies, you still must focus on building and maintaining a strong corporate reputation.

While positive brand attributes are great, telling other people you possess them isn't even half the battle. The key is to get *others* to say it about you by remaining consistent and staying true to your corporate values. Public relations and corporate promotions can help speed the evolution of your reputation. However, they can never act as a replacement for taking personal responsibility for the actions of your firm.

Defining the Brands and Relationships

Here's a quick biology lesson to get you to the core of the Balanced-Brand philosophy. People have certain hardwired traits, just as lower species are hardwired to behave in certain ways. Lions hunt. Squirrels gather. Border collies herd.

Humans relate—most everything we do is based on our standing with other people. We ask ourselves internal questions about everyone we encounter: "Do I impress you?" "Are we friends or enemies?" "Will you give me what I want?" We relate to brands in much the same way: "How do I feel about you?" "Do I agree with your values?" "What can you do for me?"

The way we relate to the products and services we buy is similar to the way we relate to each other.

At this point, you are probably saying, "This is not news. Of course the customer has a personal relationship with my brand." However, we haven't gone the next step to determine what *kind* of relationship the customer has with our product.

We sometimes forget that there are many different levels of relationships. Just because you spend all day thinking about nothing but the superior attributes of your brand, you miss the mark if you're thinking that the customer has an equally intense relationship with it.

I Just Came to Play

Most of the time, customers relate to brands the way I relate to the guys I run into at Willie's American Guitar shop. While I'll never be a great musician, my devotion to the guitar has been intact since I was eleven years old. Saturday afternoons, when I really ought to be mowing the lawn or answering e-mails, I go to Willie's. Because I've been doing this for years, I know a lot of other guitar players there.

By *know*, I mean that I can recognize their faces and attach names to them. I also realize that, just by virtue of being in the same place, we share an affinity to music in general and to guitars in particular. It's great fun to talk with people who share my passion for acoustic guitars. If we see each other at a concert or another music-related venue, we talk for a while then, too.

We share a connection based on similar interests and shared values. But ties like these are not binding, and the attachment isn't deep. So let's pretend that one of my guitar friends tells me, "I've been thinking about this for some time, and I'm going to sell my acoustic guitar, change my name to 'Slasher' and conquer the world of heavy metal."

"Hey, good luck," I might say, but we wouldn't have much to talk about any more. We aren't sharing the same musical tastes or interests; therefore we don't have a reason to continue our very casual relationship. No hard feelings, but that's the way it is.

If you're lucky, customers will feel about your brand the way I feel about the guys at Willie's—happy to see you, pleased that you have some values in common that satisfy their needs. (If you're really lucky, they will develop a genuine loyalty like fans of a rock group, but that's pretty rare.) And if your brand starts acting out of line with their values, they'll move on, usually without anyone noticing, but occasionally quite vocally.

All relationships operate on this premise: We support (spend time with, purchase products from) those whose values we share. In order to have lasting business success, you need to understand your brand's values. You need to understand the values of your stakeholders. And then you need to adjust what you're doing to line them up. Understanding the many types of values that build relationships is the basis of the power behind a thriving brand.

Brand Personality

In our personal lives, our brand messages sum up who we are:

- "I save people's lives."
- "I'm an agnostic."

- "Nothing bothers me."
- "I can make a difference."
- "I follow the rules."

These key attributes define the essence of the person. How we define ourselves gives people a glimpse of our personality. A clearly defined brand personality is imperative for stakeholders to understand the essence of your company.

Brand personality provides human characteristics that help audiences relate to your company. Here are some notions people might form based on the dimensions of your brand personality:

- *Size:* Small companies are seen as having an entrepreneurial spirit, while large companies are considered monolithic and staid.
- *Age:* Young companies might go out of business soon; older companies are not seen as innovative.
- *Category Preconceptions:* People stereotype car dealers as shady, technology companies as geeky, government organizations as slow moving—even if your particular organization is not that way.
- *Regionality:* Decisions about your brand can be based on feelings that the East Coast is pushy, the West Coast is flaky, Midwesterners are bumpkins, and Southerners are backward.

You can see how inaccurate all these generalities are, especially when applied to specific companies. Nevertheless, it's important to understand the barriers that brand builders must overcome in creating strong, clear brand personalities.

To get back to that "person-centric" theme, it's very helpful to think of your company as a person when you're creating a brand personality. Apple Computer, Target, and Budweiser have worked hard to create brand personalities that are well understood. But you don't need to be a large consumer company to have a clear brand personality.

You do need to invest time and effort to create a brand personality that's right for your firm.

Positioning

In its simplest form, positioning is sorting. Busy customers tend to group products and services by whether or not they are relevant, fit current aspirations, and are affordable. For instance, when you're looking for a car, you don't start by deciding between an Acura and a Rolls Royce. Your categories are more defined and specific, because sorting happens long before shopping, and usually before any serious thought has been given to the product or service.

As we learn about new products or services, we tend to quickly sort them into mental "short lists" for future purchase consideration. Where a brand ends up on our list—at the beginning or the end—is helped along by the work of marketers.

Three Ways to Establish a Position

There are three ways to establish your brand and reputation position:

1. *Let your customer decide who you are.* The more customers learn, the more decisions they make. Once people make up their minds, it's difficult to change their opinions, even if what they "know is true" isn't. When people don't know anything at all about a product or service, they will often ask, "What is this and how much does it cost?" This shows no real intent to buy, but merely a way to understand the relative value of something.

2. *Let your competitors tell your customers who you are.* Your competitors will gladly tell customers who you are and what you

stand for. Perhaps they will say something like, "They're a good company, but I wonder if they're still having financial difficulties," or, "I heard they were having trouble developing their next generation of products. I hope they don't leave their current customers stranded."

3. *Actively position your own brand.* By building your own position, you maximize the control and value of your brand. Creating real differentiation between your products and competitors' requires a firm understanding of your target audience. The people who buy your brand are asking themselves, "What does your product or service say about me?" In other words, "How does your product or service help me achieve my personal aspirations?"

Your brand will be positioned in the marketplace with or without your involvement. However, most successful companies carefully create and manage their brands.

Most brands never move beyond Brand Assessment—they don't make the leap to assessing and aligning values. Most companies focus solely on sales- and brand-related activities, thereby missing the essential stakeholder values assigned to your brand after the sale that play a crucial role in building a strong brand and reputation. Brand Assessment provides information necessary to assess your internal vision, values, and brand. The next step is to compare and contrast your corporate values with those of your stakeholders.

Chapter Four Summary

Brand Assessment

Brand Assessment is a comprehensive overview of an organization's vision, values, reputation, brand architecture, and position.

Vision

All organizations must have a clearly stated vision that explains why you're in business and where you're going. Without a clear vision, there cannot be values or operating procedures.

Stated Values Versus Operating Values

Stated Values are formal representations made by an organization. Operating Values are the standards and principles used every day by employees to produce and deliver goods and services.

Corporate Reputation

Reputations are built over time through actions rather than words.

Brands and Relationships

Brand loyalty is based on the level of relationship between the organization and its constituencies. Most brand relationships are easily replaced.

Brand Personality

Brand Personality describes the age, origin, size, and regionality of a brand. These traits give a common voice and image to the brand.

Positioning

Positioning is sorting. It's a mental short list customers use for grouping products and services.

There are three ways to establish a corporate position:

1. Let the customer decide who you are.
2. Let the competition tell your customers who you are.
3. Actively position your own brand.

Most companies never get beyond Brand Assessment because they are solely focused on sales and brand activities rather than values assessment and alignment.

Stakeholder Assessment

stakeholderassessment

Prioritizing Stakeholder Groups
and Assessing Stakeholder Values

Stakeholders make up the fragile ecosystem of any business.

Knowing who to nurture, who to protect, and who to avoid is the difference between thriving and facing extinction.

[Stakeholder Assessment compares and contrasts key stakeholder values with corporate values to identify opportunities and possible Flashpoints.]

Honesty, greed, power, rights, trust.

The feelings evoked by these values-based descriptions are strong enough to build enduring personal bonds or devastating enough to incite wars.

The more people care about an issue or value, the greater the intensity of reaction to others with differing views. We clash when we're convinced that only *our* set of values is right.

Low-involvement decisions, such as buying shoelaces or having a broken window fixed, rarely generate any consideration of personal values. High-involvement decisions, such as buying stock or donating to charity, are driven by personal values.

On the extreme continuum of involvement, major life decisions, like choosing medical care for your family or accepting a new job, require careful consideration of choices and connect directly to closely held values.

The values you hold and the decisions you make regarding a company or brand depend in large part on your level of involvement in the process and the type of stakeholder you are.

Identifying and Classifying Stakeholders

Each stakeholder group has its own unique profile and relationship to your company. Identifying individual stakeholder groups and classifying groups into four major categories is the first step of Stakeholder Assessment:

1. *Buyers:* Anyone who directly purchases or influences the purchase of your product or service

2. *Funders:* Investors, analysts, foundations, and private owner-ship are potential funders

3. *Builders:* Boards of directors, employees, distributors, dealers, and any other group that builds, distributes, or sells your prod-uct or service

4. *Influencers:* Community, media, industry leaders, opinion leaders, competitors, special interest groups, industry watch-dogs, and government that can impact your organization's brand and reputation

Stakeholder Identification

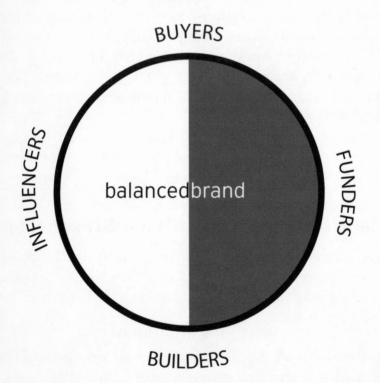

Prioritizing Stakeholder Groups

Obviously, not all stakeholder groups are equal. Ranking each group by their importance to the success of the organization is a complex process that ties directly back to your corporate values. For instance, a special interest group that has caused your company problems in the past isn't readily identified as a stakeholder. Even if they are identified, senior executives may want to rank them as a low priority based on an emotional reaction rather than a strategic business reality. Establishing objective criteria for identifying and prioritizing stakeholder groups is imperative to managing your brand and reputation.

On a Mission   Bill George is the former CEO of Medtronic, the world's leading medical technology company. His book, *Authentic Leadership*,[1] demonstrates that mission-driven organizations experience the best performance over time. While managing Medtronic, George incurred the ire of Wall Street by proclaiming that Medtronic ranked stakeholders in this order:

1. Customers
2. Employees
3. Shareholders

In an age of immense shareholder influence, placing employees ahead of shareholders was viewed as blasphemous. However, George understood that employee commitment to Medtronic's mission of "restoring life" would build long-term value for all stakeholders. Based on the company's performance, it's clear his hierarchy of stakeholders and mission were right for Medtronic.

Every Stakeholder Has an Agenda

While every stakeholder brings a unique set of values to bear on your brand, your job is to weigh them against your own corporate priorities. You need to move beyond being strictly customer and shareholder focused to understanding how *all* stakeholders affect the success of the company.

With the overall responsibility of running a company, you know it's impossible to be all things to all stakeholders. By their very nature, stakeholders' values and agendas are quite different. Like Bill George, you need to create your own hierarchy of stakeholder importance with the intent of creating and maintaining a balanced brand. And you need to know that no matter what decision you make, there will be some conflict because of it. Your goal is to contain conflict, avoid backlash, and build a strong brand and strong reputation in spite of the pressure of business and market forces.

Purchasing a product or service, starting a new job, purchasing a stock all mark the beginning of a brand relationship. You may aspire to buy the newest product, but you don't assign values until you've had direct experience with the brand. Employees often change jobs as a result of career aspirations, only to find that job satisfaction is much more strongly tied to corporate environment than to salaries or titles.

Using Stakeholder Assessment, you can continually monitor and take advantage of shifts in stakeholder values that not only affect sales but also loyalty.

Most people's political, social, and religious values have no bearing on your business. Isolating stakeholder values that directly influence your business is the goal of our model.

We've identified three dimensions of stakeholder values that are interrelated in shaping attitudes and opinions about a company's brand and reputation. By sorting stakeholder values into these three dimensions, you are able to systematically analyze multiple stakeholder groups.

The Three Dimensions of the Values Pyramid

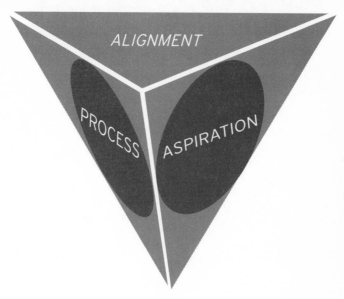

The three dimensions of the Values Pyramid are defined as:

1. *Aspiration:* How well does the company's product or service satisfy a stakeholder's needs and desires?
2. *Process:* How well does the product manufacturing process or service delivery process achieve the expected standard performance?
3. *Impact:* What is the impact of your product or service on the community or environment?

Managing Stakeholder Values

Stakeholder values that are plotted on the top two points of the Values Pyramid represent *alignment* and stability. Values that are plotted toward the bottom of the Values Pyramid can create instability that can pull a company out of balance, resulting in *Flashpoints*. A Flashpoint represents a critical threshold for stakeholder alignment. If your company has crossed that threshold, you risk backlash in the form of boycotts, lawsuits, strikes, or government intervention.

Knowing exactly where stakeholder values fall on the Values Pyramid provides the insights necessary for your organization to manage each stakeholder group most effectively.

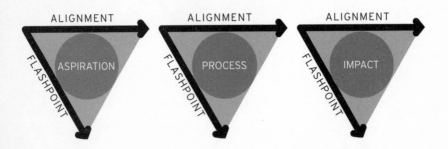

Stakeholder Assessment identifies stakeholder values and provides a framework for understanding the reaction a company can expect from each stakeholder given a particular decision or action. Depending on the importance of the stakeholder group, your company will choose to:

- Align corporate values with stakeholder values
- Manage stakeholder expectations
- Monitor stakeholder reactions

By using the model effectively and repeatedly, you can make more right decisions and perhaps avoid wrong ones.

Note: To simplify the stakeholder values examples, we have chosen to use the "customer" to illustrate Stakeholder Assessment because they are the most common of all key stakeholder groups. However, values assessments of employees, community, government, and investors are the only ways to provide a useful management tool for your company. Plotting stakeholder values for each group is the only way to gain a clear understanding of the crucial issues impacting your business.

Aspiration

I've always dreamed of . . . By the time you're a year old, your life is filled with aspirations. You want cookies instead of carrots, playtime instead of bedtime. You quickly learn how to act in order to get what you want.

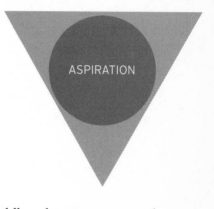

To a child, Happy Meals are the desired item, not because McDonald's has great or nutritious food, but because the meals come with a toy. Their childhood aspirations are the same forces that directly lead to the fifty-year-old "kid," fueled by a lifelong desire for a dream machine, purchasing a Porsche as basic transportation.

These territories are so well charted in our business world that it seems easy to write a strategic plan and execute the plan on time and on budget—never mind if it actually works. There are many companies, regardless of size, that still fail to successfully market their products or services because getting to the heart of the right aspirations requires greater insights than simply listing features and benefits. Aspiration values can be very elusive and ever changing. What worked last year may be exactly the wrong strategy moving forward because of rapidly changing business environment and evolving values.

Companies are learning that values play a pivotal role in driving aspirational behavior. The simplicity of creating or fulfilling needs or experiences does not account for many of the closely held values that are at the center of most stakeholder behavior. Career aspirations of learning new skills, doing important work, or feeling appreciated can make significant impact on satisfaction and performance of your employees.

Investing in companies you trust or are proud to own directly influences investor loyalty and support. Being an involved, caring community leader can make the difference between strong community support or grassroots opposition to your organization.

Aspiration—every stakeholder group has its own unique set of aspirational values. Identifying your customer's aspirational values is crucial to success. Looking beyond the customer for understanding of how all stakeholder aspirational values affect your business creates a powerful competitive advantage.

What Are the Aspirations of Buying a Watch?

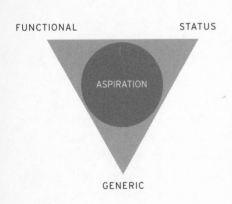

Let's pretend you own a watch manufacturing company.

Determining the values necessary to sell your watches competitively depends on your stakeholders. Since the introduction of quartz movements, all watches keep essentially accurate time. So what differentiates one wristwatch from another? Not the watch or the watch manufacturer, but rather buyers and their aspirations.

If owning a wristwatch is meaningless to your customer beyond knowing the time, he or she will buy an inexpensive *generic* watch from a convenience store and throw it away when it breaks.

If your customer is a runner or a scuba diver, she will buy a watch that offers the *functional* performance and the quality necessary so that she can enjoy her sport.

If your customer feels as if a wristwatch helps define his values on workmanship or prestige, then purchasing a watch from a fine jewelry store signals the *status* that he is seeking.

In each case, the purchasing decision is based on how the watch reflects your customer's lifestyle and values. As marketers, we've done an excellent job of understanding and defining the purchasing habits of our customers. The next step is examining our brands after purchase, as customers begin to assign their personal values to the products they own.

[How does buying your product or service reflect my values?]

Status on the Cheap

Not all status purchases necessarily cost a lot. In fact, contemporary lifestyle trackers note a growing group of mid-income consumers who "trade up" in a certain product category in return for a treat that helps the consumer feel better—about themselves, their social status, or their self-image.[2] High-rising brands in this category include Victoria's Secret, Godiva Chocolate, or microbrewery beers like Samuel Adams.[3]

Are Business-to-Business Purchases Rational?

The emotional impact of how people feel about buying your product or service weighs heavily in both first-time purchases and long-term loyalty. This impact is just as valid in business-to-business as in consumer brand decisions. There's a notion that once a purchaser gets to the office, emotional consumer behaviors are left behind, and they become a totally rational buyer. But B-to-B buyers are the same stressed-out nuts who were fighting road rage on their way to work. Pulling into the parking lot and walking into the office doesn't give them any additional edge of rationality.

There's another factor that can complicate things in this segment. If your B-to-B brand is relatively unknown, the risk of buying from an unknown company is high. No one was ever fired for selecting IBM, McKinsey, or Steelcase. If the procurement person didn't select the best-known brand, there is usually a very strong rationale for the decision. If your brand is weak or unknown, it's your job to provide compelling advantages and rationale to make the buyer feel comfortable recommending your product or service.

Twenty Percent Is All It Would Take

A recent research study asked people how much more money they would need to feel good about retirement. The answer was "about 20% more than I'm currently making."[4,5] It didn't matter how much money people already had—everyone felt that if they just had 20% more, they would be all right.

Most of us would like 20% more of everything—20% more time or 20% more stuff or a 20% larger house at a 20% discount. How about 20% more exercise? In the minds of most people, 20% is an achievable goal without making them feel greedy.

There is a downside to the 20% rule, however. When fast food restaurants started to increase food portions by 20%, people readily bought the super-sized portions, and now we're faced with a national obesity problem. Most values can be double edged. Marketers must carefully examine the personal, professional, and social ramifications of aligning with stakeholder values. The old axiom, "too much of a good thing," has never been more true.

Once a purchase is made, the new owner attempts to identify the relevance and aspirations underlying the purchase. This is an opportunity for a deeper level of a brand relationship. At an unconscious level, the assignment of new personal values to the brand also begins. Like customers, employees and shareholders assign additional values such as job satisfaction or social responsibility because they have a vested interest in how your company performs.

Process and impact become important dimensions of your brand after a purchasing decision because they reflect how your products or services are expected to work in accordance with owners' values. This is where BalancedBrand becomes vital in maintaining your brand position. You must understand the relationship among aspirations, process, and impact in order to build and maintain strong stakeholder loyalty.

[A new level of brand relationship begins after a purchase is made.]

Process

Made and delivered the way I want . . .

The process of how a product is made or a service is delivered has become increasingly important. Quality, speed, competition, and cost are all critical dimensions of process.

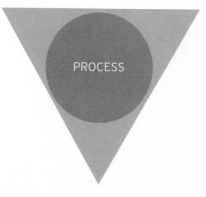

Quality and price are no longer an either/or proposition. While Americans worry and complain about outsourcing, we've come to expect higher and higher quality at lower costs. The mantra among most CEOs is to either "take out costs or increase value" in order to compete. Global competition has forced companies to completely reevaluate their manufacturing and service processes. Streamlined operating processes and outsourcing have already accounted for most available cost reduction; therefore, adding value through service and quality are today's key differentiators.

Stakeholders adapt quickly to new technology and expect increasingly higher levels of performance all the time. Until Federal Express came along, no one even considered sending or receiving a package overnight. Now we absolutely expect our package the next day.

The FedEx example demonstrates how each time a new level of service is achieved, it quickly becomes the standard and is no longer exceptional. Trying to create a differentiated, competitive advantage requires continual innovation and continuous improvement. The only way to get there is by knowing your stakeholders' expectations and having your employees on your side.

The implications for the people who make the product or deliver the service can become very personal. Their actions will either build or destroy stakeholder relationships. While process is judged according to the end user's values, those most directly affected by Process Values are the employees who spend the day tightening screws, answering the phone, or serving the customer.

Returning to the watch example, we can see how process affects the personal values of the customer. If your customer bought a generic watch from a convenience store, chances are she won't care how it was manufactured, much less who made the watch. Her primary concern is cost, not whether the manufacturer used Third World labor practices or *outsourced* jobs for cheaper cost of goods.

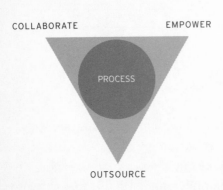

COLLABORATE   EMPOWER

PROCESS

OUTSOURCE

If he bought a functional watch from a sporting goods store, your customer is concerned about the quality of the manufacturing process. He expects reasonable craftsmanship and therefore a *collaborative* work environment that sustains his expected level of quality.

If your customer bought a status watch from a fine jewelry store, she would expect the manufacturer to hire the most skilled designers and craftspeople available who are *empowered* to design a one-of-a-kind, world-class timepiece.

In each case, the long-term success of the brand relationship depends on the relationship between Aspiration and Process. Success is directly correlated to both. Aspiration gives stakeholders what they want. Process delivers goods and services in the way that fits their values.

There are many times when the role of process isn't as evident in its effect on customer satisfaction. It may be months or even years after the purchase of a product that the quality of the manufacturing becomes apparent. Recalls can occur long after the original launch, but can still have a devastating effect on the company's reputation.

Worst Job

What was the worst job you ever had? Everyone seems to have a great answer to this question. In fact, without having a couple of really bad jobs, it's difficult to appreciate a good job.

When I was fourteen years old, I was hired at a very exclusive country club as a pot washer. This first rung on my career ladder paid $1.14 an hour, which, even in the dark ages of my youth, was not a handsome sum. I was still excited because it was a "real job."

I started on Sunday at 6 A.M. The morning chef led me into a room with a large stainless steel sink piled to the ceiling with last night's dirty, crusty, baked-on pots. It looked like a scene from a sit-uation comedy, except for the fact that the joke was on me. Hand-ing me a bottle of skin-removing-strength detergent and a pair of rubber gloves, he told me to let him know when I was caught up.

That never happened. By the time I got the pots scrubbed from the night before, the breakfast pots were waiting for me. By the time I finished the breakfast pots, lunch was over. I finally dragged myself out of the kitchen at four o'clock that afternoon, feeling raw but also exhilarated by the prospect of earning my own money. I was happy, and my employer was happy.

The question is, would any of the members of the country club have cared that a fourteen-year-old had been hired in the kitchen at well below minimum wage? While this was cheap labor for the management and satisfaction for me, there could have been a differing view from the government or some of the club's members. Back then no one cared or noticed. However, personal and community values have dramatically changed the employment landscape. While our economy is built on cheap labor, we must be ever vigilant of understanding the stakeholders' values and aligning with their expectations for how a product is made or how a service is delivered.

Simplicity as a Value

Many companies have equated added functionality with added value. Competing companies have created a "features frenzy" without consideration for their time-starved, stressed-out customers. When listening to any sales pitch on the latest features and benefits, we are thinking, "I don't care if my cell phone has global positioning, games, appointment book, and camera; I just want to make a call. Why does everything have to be so hard?" We need lessons to learn how to operate our cell phones, computers, software, television, DVD players, and even our cars.

Complexity also has a profound negative effect on productivity in the workplace. Billions of dollars worth of software applications sit on the shelf collecting dust because people haven't been adequately trained or haven't taken the time to learn how to use the software. What looked great in the demo has no resemblance to the real world.

Companies that recognize the need for simplicity as a process value have significant competitive advantage over those companies who continue to add complexity instead of added value.

They Care More Than You Think: The Nike Example

As in most large organizations, business philosophy is to improve profits and quality while reducing costs. At Nike, this philosophy backfired. Nike selected the cheapest source of labor to manufacture quality athletic footwear. While adding quality and reducing costs would appear to have been the most important job of the manufacturer, the *number 1* job was to stay in alignment with key stakeholder values, and that's where the disconnect happened. Nike never understood the personal values of a significant group of customers and stakeholders, thereby damaging its brand and reputation. Process matters, and, to some stakeholders, it's all that matters.

Ten years after the story broke about Nike using sweatshops to manufacture its athletic footwear, people still have not forgotten and often associate the word *Nike* with the word *sweatshop* in market research studies.[6] Even though Nike has changed many of its labor practices, this is one story that still haunts them.

[
It's dangerous to your brand and reputation to assume that the only product attributes people are interested in are price or quality. Ask Nike.
]

The McKinsey Proposal

The McKinsey Global Institute, a think tank of McKinsey & Co., has recommended that companies sending jobs abroad contribute about 5% of their savings to an insurance fund that would compensate displaced workers for part of the difference in wages paid by their old and new jobs. While this proposal has merit, most companies are facing price barriers and are burdened by escalating health care and defined benefits costs. However, the goodwill generated by finding 5% may be the right solution for some companies.[7]

Contraction . . . On Demand

IBM Global Services announced in May 2005 a workforce reduction of 13,000 people. Because of national trade practices, the cost for the company to reduce its workforce in Germany and the UK was expected to be $1.3 billion–$1.7 billion.[8] As most CEOs of global companies are painfully aware, each country has its own standards for labor practices. These standards can have a chilling effect on job creation because of the high penalties companies must pay in order to respond to global competition. National labor practices increasingly play a larger role in job creation. The conundrum for most senior managers is balancing between market expansion and the backlash associated with market contraction. There are no easy solutions to addressing the complexities and demands of global competition. Those who have lost their jobs to outsourcing rightfully feel like the victims of global trade.

Understanding stakeholder Process Values will make your decision-making path clearer. Unfortunately, each stakeholder group is becoming more polarized in their views and values on process.

Impact

Don't mess with my world . . .

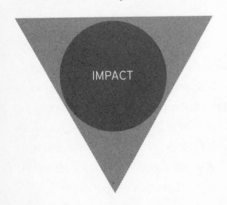

Communities—they may be geographic or user communities, but in either case the impact a product or service has on a community can have a profound affect on your brand and reputation. Many of the most influential brand and reputation discussions take place online among user groups that are outside your control. Understanding how business decisions impact the community or environment is crucial to aligning your values with stakeholder values. What looks like a great economic business decision can, when placed against environmental or community repercussions, have devastating consequences for your company's brand and reputation. Knowing exactly where your stakeholders stand on decisions affecting the community or environment helps you make the right call.

How strongly stakeholders feel about the impact a company has on the environment or community depends on their relationship with the company and its direct impact on their lives. You already know that, for the watch purchaser, value dimensions of Aspiration and Process are related.

The same is true for Impact. Once again, if your customer purchases a generic watch, he or she probably has little or no expectations about what resources may have been *depleted* to make the watch, or if any toxic waste might come from the components or battery. However, if she bought a functional watch designed for running or scuba, she may expect your company to *sustain* her sport through local event sponsorships and to have responsible environmental policies based on her personal values. Part of the status of your customer's owning an expensive watch may be derived from the company's participation in *improving* his community or environment by sponsoring a favorite charity or by demonstrating strong environmental stewardship.

Issues such as jobs versus the environment have been around for years. What's different is how individuals, communities, and governments are reacting to these issues. With the advent of the Internet, creating global communities around special interests is as easy as posting a

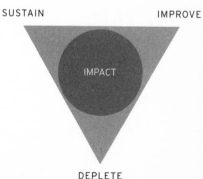

Web site. Business no longer has the same influence or control over communities because many communities of users are established outside the sphere of the company. By doing a comprehensive search on the Internet, you can find out how people feel about a company's products, environmental record, philanthropic activities, work environment, corporate culture, business performance, financial analysis, and even rumors. A significant portion of this information comes directly from stakeholders, former employees, and competitors.

The Internet has made user groups a powerful constituency. Users tend to trust the opinions of other users over company-sponsored information. They can log online and instantly discuss the merits and faults of a product or service. Sharing information such as costs, performance, quality, and service with current and prospective users creates a public forum. These groups love to let companies know where they stand and what they expect.

States and local government also have a stronger voice in corporate affairs. Lawsuits have been brought by state attorneys general. Class action suits by consumers or employees have become commonplace. Local governments offer generous incentives for companies to create community-based jobs, but the same governments can be very aggressive in pursuing companies believed to be harmful to their communities.

Who Owns Your Computer?

When you bought your computer, future disposal of your laptop was surely the last thing on your mind. You cared about memory, display features, and price. But your computer is full of toxic waste, and how to dispose of it—and thousands of other out-of-date cell phones, VCRs, and discarded techno-junk—is a major issue facing communities and countries. Finding responsible ways to dispose of toxic materials has become a very complex international problem. Some nations now require manufacturers to be responsible for disposing of their products. This is called "lifetime ownership."

When you're done using your computer, companies like Dell or Gateway are responsible for breaking down the components and properly recycling or disposing of the waste. Consumers pay for the use of the product, and manufacturers include an additional cost to dispose of the product.

For the Price of a Cup of Coffee

The price of coffee worldwide is plummeting. This may be good news at the grocery store, but it's bad news for coffee growers in Guatemala, Ecuador, and Mexico. For centuries, they have been growing coffee in the shade of the forest canopy. Coffee workers harvest ripe, red fruits—appropriately called cherries—by hand. The cherries contain Arabica beans, which produce the richest coffee in the world. The plummeting crop price threatens the livelihood of an estimated 20 million people in fifty countries.[9]

Because of the price drop, there has been a drastic change in agricultural practices for growing and harvesting coffee beans in Asia. Coffee in that region is being produced by clearing land and growing coffee beans in open fields, which leads to lower-quality beans and which ultimately destroys the land. More coffee can be grown this way, stabilizing incomes that are shrinking with bean prices.

The question becomes, how many people care where their coffee comes from or what impact it has on the growers and environment? Are we willing to pay more for coffee grown with sustainable methods? If so, how much?

Designed to Sustain

Many innovative businesses and universities are looking at design as the solution for our environmental and community challenges. If a product or service is designed to reduce the amount of energy and waste associated with production and consumption, everyone wins. By focusing on conservation at the beginning of the process, as opposed to the end of the process, we get such products as hybrid cars, recycled paper, phosphate-free detergent, long-life light bulbs, and paperless billing. That's just the beginning. Smart building materials, solar power, and sustainable agriculture make good economic sense. Efforts among businesses, local communities, and conservationists seeking practical solutions to global problems are on the rise. Our collective design and engineering capabilities provide the opportunities for any business to create a competitive advantage by investing in long-term sustainability.

Community-Level Investment

Smart investment in communities not only builds loyalty, but it also can result in enormous economic and reputation windfalls. There are numerous stories of companies reinvesting in struggling local communities to create safer, more attractive neighborhoods, training programs, and community outreach surrounding their headquarters, which attracts and retain quality workers.

One example from the world of sports is the Memphis Redbirds baseball team, whose brand slogan is "Baseball is our business . . . but the community is our bottom line."

A farm team of the St. Louis Cardinals, the Redbirds are the only not-for-profit sports team and facility in the United States. The Redbirds team was founded by Dean Jernigan, chairman, president, CEO, and founder of Storage USA Inc., the country's second-largest self-storage operation. Jernigan, a Memphis native, saw baseball as part of the community and a way to connect to something greater than himself. Looking at Memphis's history of desertion by professional sports teams, he decided to create a team that would improve, and not deplete, the surrounding community.

All team operating profits are put back into The Memphis Redbirds Baseball Foundation, which funds two youth programs: RBI (Returning Baseball to the Inner City) and STRIPES (Sports

Teams Returning In the Public Education System). These programs foster amateur sports, enhance education, and teach life skills for the future.

Jernigan's core business principles are worth reviewing:

- Just because something could be a business doesn't mean that it should be a business.
- Just because something isn't a business doesn't mean that it can't be run like a business.
- Predictable plans lead to expected outcomes. And doing the unpredictable often leads to extraordinary outcomes.
- Good ideas don't always win—at least not at first.
- What is least glamorous is often most gratifying.

The Redbirds have transcended local entertainment by becoming part of the social fabric of the community. The entire Memphis area and St. Louis Cardinals organization benefits from the philanthropic vision of Jernigan.[10]

One Hundred Years of Coming Home

Andersen Corporation recently celebrated its 100-year anniversary by committing to help Habitat for Humanity build 100 homes over a five-year period. Andersen has a long history of giving back to the community. From community service projects to encouraging employee volunteerism, Andersen has built a reputation for social responsibility and leadership. As the largest window and door manufacturer in America, Andersen has instituted a remarkable profit-sharing program that allows all employees to participate in the company's success. On the environmental front, Andersen was one of the first manufacturers to give preference for FSC-certified lumber standards, based on ecologically, socially, and economically sustainable forest management.[11] As Andersen Windows' slogan proclaims, "Come Home to Andersen" demonstrates what it means to live your brand.

Identifying and sorting stakeholder values by Aspiration, Process, and Impact will help your organization determine specific departmental responsibility. Once you have identified your unique set of corporate and stakeholder values, sorting each value and stakeholder group into the three parameters of aspiration, process, and impact becomes self-evident.

This sorting process makes the management and responsibility of each value in your stakeholder group easy for your organization to assimilate.

1. Aspiration values typically fall under the responsibility of marketing.

2. Process values are usually related to operational functions.

3. Impact values are typically managed through the area of social responsibility. Many organizations use corporate communications or have no formal group assigned internally to manage social responsibility.

Understanding exactly who is responsible in your organization for specific stakeholder values creates the accountability necessary to effectively manage these activities.

Measuring return on investment and isolating which values are most likely to drive behavior is the next phase of stakeholder assessment.

Chapter Five Summary

The more people care about a particular issue or value, the greater the intensity of reaction to others with differing views.

Identifying and Prioritizing Stakeholder Groups

Identifying and prioritizing each Stakeholder Group is the starting point of Stakeholder Assessment.

Stakeholder Agendas

Each Stakeholder Group has a unique and sometimes conflicting set of values:

- Buyers care about how a product or service will fulfill their aspirations and personal values.
- Funders are interested in maximizing shareholder value.
- Builders care about work environment and doing important work.
- Influencers are concerned with social or economic impact, job creation, and the environment.

Stakeholder agendas identify, prioritize, and measure key stakeholder values against your corporate values to guide strategic decision making that propels future success.

Stakeholder Assessment Pyramid

1. Aspiration: How well does the company's product or service satisfy a purchaser's needs and desires?
2. Process: Does the product manufacturing process or service delivery reflect the expected standard levels set by all stakeholders?
3. Impact: How does the product or service positively or negatively affect the community or the environment?

Stakeholder Return on Investment

Measuring Values That Drive Behavior and Your Bottom Line

Blind faith is an unwelcome interloper
in free markets.

If you can't measure it . . . it doesn't exist.

Investing in values and outcomes that demonstrate a tangible benefit for your organization fuels The Balanced Brand System. In the previous chapter, we identified the stakeholders and values and dimensions that drive business. In this chapter we measure the impact of stakeholders' values on behavior and business performance. Using the metrics outlined here, you'll be able to quantify outcomes and calibrate future business actions.

3R Brand Equation

Alignment with stakeholder values must show measurable outcomes. The return on investment (ROI) may be measured as a direct benefit to the stakeholder as well as demonstrating financial performance. Alignment outcomes can be identified and measured by using the 3R Brand Equation. For employees, the equation refers to Return on *Involvement* instead of Investment. While there are monetary incentives for performance, there is also the personal benefit, which is a major factor in employee satisfaction.

The 3R Brand Equation is designed to measure the following:

Relevance + Relationship = Return on Investment

Relevance: For the stakeholder, what need is fulfilled by the brand, product, or service?

Relationship: How do the values of the organization align with those of the stakeholder?

Return on Investment: What is the outcome as measured in direct benefit or financial returns?

Return on Involvement: What are the direct benefits for supporting the organization's values? Return on Involvement more accurately reflects the values of the Builders stakeholder group. Employees are looking for job satisfaction, career growth, and positive work environment in addition to wages and benefits.

The 3R Brand Equation provides the critical information necessary to identify and evaluate which stakeholder values impact outcomes. Within the equation, the importance and intensity of the stakeholder values are correlated to the relevance and relationships that deliver the corresponding ROI. If there is no measurable outcome, why invest resources to achieve alignment? All three values dimensions—Aspiration, Process, and Impact—are interdependent in the 3R Brand Equation. Focusing on ROI is essential to building meaningful values metrics. As a result, your organization will be able to measure and calibrate its actions based on stakeholder values alignment.

The following is a composite example drawn from real-world experiences of a number of our clients in the health care industry. We have used their stakeholder values in the 3R Brand Equation to demonstrate outcomes and ROI.

This example illustrates the importance of understanding physicians' needs and values (ongoing product information and training) combined with the manufacturers' willingness to align with these

Example of 3R Brand Equation (Business Category: Medical Devices; Stakeholder Group: Physicians)

Relevance	+	Relationship	=	Return on Investment
Want a proven device		Physicians: Provides ongoing, clear, concise product data		Reduced risk for the manufacturer and physician
		Device manufacturer: Provides full disclosure		
Want easier, faster implanting procedure		Physicians: Train me in latest procedures and technology		Less invasive procedure, resulting in competitive advantage
		Device manufacturer: Offer in-field collaboration		

needs and values (full disclosure, training, and collaboration). Reducing risk allows the company to increase market share, enhance its reputation, and mitigate legal liability. Providing training on a less invasive procedure increases loyalty among physicians. These outcomes are measurable and directly relate to ROI.

By going through the rigor of ensuring that the alignment of corporate values with stakeholder values has a measurable outcome, you can determine the benefit of values driven activities.

Stakeholders' Values Maps

The three dimensions of the Values Pyramid help categorize values, but they do not provide adequate insights as to how strongly these stakeholder values are held. Values Maps are designed to measure the intensity of specific values by identifying and quantifying them as either Dominant or Latent Values for each stakeholder group. Each stakeholder group's values are sorted by the dimensions of Aspiration, Process, and Impact. Values Maps then determine which values will most likely drive behavior.

By comparing the Dominant and Latent Values of each group, we can provide a clear picture of how stakeholders' values cluster in relation to each other and the company. This information is invaluable for strategic planning and crisis intervention. The following is an example of a Values Map.

Dominant Values

Stakeholders hold an array of personal values that affect behaviors, attitudes, and purchasing decisions. A Dominant Value is one that overrides other values or attributes. These can either build or destroy brands and reputations. For instance, personal values such as health, family, money, faith, self-esteem, and safety are obvious Dominant Values. These values evoke the strongest emotions and reactions from stakeholders.

Stakeholders' Values Map

High Involvement Latent Value	High Involvement Dominant Value
Low Involvement Latent Value	Low Involvement Dominant Value

INVOLVEMENT

VALUE DOMINANCE

Many people vote in elections based on one issue. Regardless of other considerations or influences, Dominant Values are the only factors that matter to some stakeholders. Environment, community, quality, labor, and ethics may be either Dominant or Latent Values depending on the stakeholder and circumstance.

The challenge arises when two stakeholder groups hold opposing Dominant Values. Management may not be able to appease one group without alienating the other. However, determining which stakeholder group is most important and acting quickly to diffuse a potential conflict can turn the makings of disaster into an opportunity to strengthen relationships.

Latent Values

Latent Values shape opinions and attitudes in more subtle ways. These are the values stakeholders care about, but that tend not to change behavior. Issues such as community involvement, foreign ownership, and lingering environmental concerns are examples of values that stakeholders may show more ambivalence toward. However, Latent Values tend to affect brands and reputations over time.

Latent Values can also rise to importance and create backlash. These values can shift to dominance or combine with other Latent Values and become a deciding factor for action by a particular stakeholder group.

Years of isolated employee labor problems culminated into a larger challenge—a class action lawsuit brought against Wal-Mart by their female employees. Fair wages alone were not enough to trigger action for the female employees of Wal-Mart. However, with the value of fair wage combined with other labor issues, Latent Values shifted to a dominant position and caused a Flashpoint, resulting in the group taking legal action.

Flashpoints

Stakeholders' level of involvement is in direct proportion to how strongly they feel about a set of values. There is a point where a culmination of issues (such as product or service experiences, quality of workmanship or service, labor practices, and community or environmental impact) creates a situation that causes a Flashpoint. These incidents incite a serious reevaluation of attitudes and behaviors toward a company, product, or service.

Some major Flashpoints, such as an outbreak of war, a Supreme Court ruling, economic downturns, or a national election, can cause a sea change in values and attitudes. Sometimes Flashpoints are caused by a collective set of personal experiences, either positive or negative, that provoke a reevaluation of values alignment with a company's product or service.

Understanding the intersection of conflicting values among stakeholder groups and your organization while measuring the importance of each value to the stakeholder group will help you recognize potential Flashpoints and determine their origin. Identifying and monitoring stakeholder values on the threshold of a Flashpoint or immediately following a Flashpoint can create a significant competitive advantage.

Methodology

Stakeholder Assessment combines qualitative and quantitative research models based on the size of the stakeholder base. The qualitative research consists of one-on-one interviews with representative key stakeholders. These interviews are used to identify and rank Dominant and Latent Values.

To ensure that the responses from the research accurately represent the thoughts and feelings of an entire stakeholder group, we recommend the use of quantitative research methods. Quantitative research provides statistical models that can predict the reliability of answers based on the number of respondents surveyed (typically 300 or more key stakeholders).

Returning to the example of ROI for medical devices, plotting the value reveals both its degree of involvement and intensity. By comparing and contrasting identified stakeholder value responses, you can create a baseline for monitoring key stakeholder values.

Monitoring Changing Values

Consumer confidence fluctuates every month. Business cycles are continually changing. Economic and world events are powerful and unpredictable forces that influence stakeholder values.

Composite Medical Device Company (Stakeholder: Physicians)

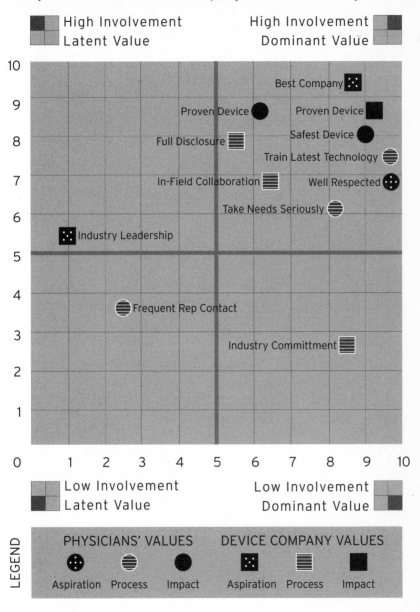

High Involvement
Latent Value

High Involvement
Dominant Value

Best Company

Proven Device

Proven Device

Full Disclosure

Safest Device

Train Latest Technology

In-Field Collaboration

Well Respected

Take Needs Seriously

Industry Leadership

Frequent Rep Contact

Industry Committment

Low Involvement
Latent Value

Low Involvement
Dominant Value

LEGEND

PHYSICIANS' VALUES   DEVICE COMPANY VALUES

Aspiration   Process   Impact   Aspiration   Process   Impact

Organizations cannot rely on tired anecdotes and war stories about "what the customer really wants." Continuously measuring and monitoring an array of stakeholder values provides a more accurate and robust platform from which to run your business. Using this platform, your organization can define an acceptable range to achieve alignment, from which your company can build its brand and reputation.

Values Monitoring

Factiva, a joint venture of Dow Jones & Reuters, has developed a proprietary Insight monitoring system designed specifically to monitor and report shifting stakeholder values identified by its clients. Factiva Insight currently monitors more than 9,000 media outlets, more than 11,000 Web sites, and 1.6 million of the most active blogs to deliver customized reporting on a daily, weekly, or monthly basis. When an issue, shifting value, or Flashpoint is identified, Values monitoring delivers critical information in timely, actionable reports.

Continuous monitoring provides the opportunity to identify changing values and trends before the competition does. It also ensures that you have all the vital competitive, consumer, and stakeholder information necessary for making important business and marketing decisions. Achieving and maintaining balance depends on having accurate stakeholder value information.

Using Stakeholder Assessment, we have examined how to identify, prioritize, and accurately assess corporate stakeholder values. Now you have the information necessary to initiate corporate and stakeholder alignment, the second part of BalancedBrand.

Chapter Six Summary

3R Brand Equation
The 3R Brand Equation examines each stakeholder value based on relevance and relationship to determine the ROI. Your organization has a unique set of values, and therefore the 3R Brand Equation will vary. Once the ROI is determined, a monetary metric can be established for each outcome.

Stakeholder Values Maps
While the Stakeholder Assessment Pyramid categorizes stakeholder values, Stakeholder Values Maps measure the intensity (Dominant and Latent Values) of each value by stakeholder group.

Dominant and Latent Values
The stakeholder values that are important to measure are those that directly impact behavior, known as Dominant Values. Latent Values are those values that are potentially important to stakeholders but have not yet been acted upon. They can move into dominance at any time, or combine to become dominant, thus affecting behavior. Latent Values are important to measure because of their potential to become dominant.

Flashpoints
A Flashpoint can be a problem or opportunity, depending on how well you've monitored stakeholder values while on the threshold of a Flashpoint and afterward.

Methodology
The methodology of mapping dominant and latent stakeholder values includes qualitative and quantitative research.

Values Monitoring

Values monitoring system delivers continuous, customized reports that identify changing values and trends ahead of the competition.

Stakeholder Assessment provides a framework to understand what reaction you can expect as a result of a particular decision or action.

part two

Alignment of Organization and Stakeholder Values

Balanced Culture

balancedculture

Changing Your Company to Align with Stakeholders

Tradition Versus Change

Change Versus Stagnation

Stagnation Versus Culture Clash

Culture Clash Versus Shared Values

Competition demands that business change
the product, change the service, even change the
culture. . . . Values are the one constant in great
companies.

[Balanced Culture embraces the power of aligning corporate values with stakeholder values.]

One of the biggest fears for most senior executives is that employees won't respond to a new vision or direction for the company. In the executive's nightmare scenario, the senior team is running ahead and shouting, "Follow us to the promised land!"—and the whole organization takes a wait-and-see attitude.

The fear is valid. Some, if not most, people resist change. Change is uncomfortable and disruptive. It's no wonder some people adamantly oppose it. Even when the survival of the company is on the line, many people struggle to change course.

That is why challenges like meeting impossible deadlines, working with shrinking budgets, and satisfying increasingly demanding customers seem manageable in comparison to moving the mountain of an entire organization to a new path. In many cases, companies fail to meet the challenge. All too often, the default strategy for instituting real change simply becomes an overhaul of the corporate identity. The new vision is embodied in a new visual identity and slogan and is rolled out in a slick, expensive new advertising campaign. This is the equivalent of doing a new paint job on an old, damaged car. It looks good, but it doesn't run any better.

Change Versus Evolution

In the context of corporate cultures, most of us think of change as being episodic. It portends an arduous, high-risk series of events, undertaken when the pain or the uncertainty of the future forces our hand. No wonder change gets such a bad rap. We suggest replacing the term *change* with the term *evolution*. While the marketplace changes rapidly, even daily, meaningful shifts in external communities, governments, and environments evolve over time.

Cultures that look beyond today's marketplace and foster a steady and long-term evolution will be highly rewarded. Without evolution, it is impossible to create and maintain balance.

Balanced Culture depends on your viewpoint. We all know the customer is king, but other key stakeholders influence success as well. This is why management teams must look beyond brand management that is purely customer focused. Balanced Brand cannot exist without Balanced Culture. Without the minds and hearts of the employees, balance is impossible. Only by taking into consideration all stakeholders can executives effectively manage the conflicting values and agendas that drive their business.

Stakeholder Advocates and Adversaries

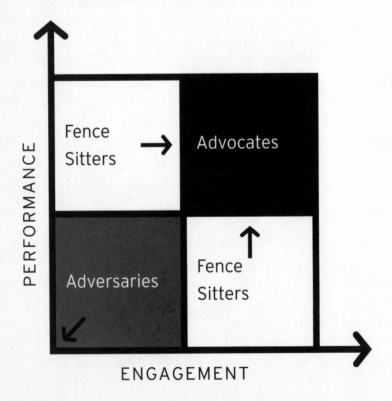

Building Advocates

The Stakeholder Advocates and Adversaries Chart measures the threshold necessary to achieve behavioral stakeholder change. It is impossible for your company to align stated and operating values without a significant group of employee advocates in your organization. Measuring advocates, adversaries, and fence sitters is critical to understanding the health of your corporate culture. Once you've identified advocates, adversaries, and fence sitters, the challenge is to eliminate the adversaries and convert the fence sitters. Advocates can help drive change within the organization. Adversaries are most often a toxic influence. Knowing the difference is a key to change management.

Balanced Culture begins with your whole organization understanding the importance of aligning your operating values with stakeholder values. Buy-in occurs when employees recognize the opportunities and threats created by alignment versus flashpoints. Advocates are the catalyst for building meaningful, lasting change.

The Evolving Culture

Balanced Culture creates a comprehensive plan that reaches every level of your organization. The ultimate goal is to align your organization's values and your stakeholders' values.

Here are some guidelines for creating and sustaining Balanced Culture:

- Ensure that you have a clear and accurate picture of your current corporate culture.
- Conduct an in-depth review of how well your corporate culture aligns with stakeholder-assigned values.
- Review your corporate vision and operating values to identify possible gaps between your organization's and your stakeholders' values.

- Get buy-in from senior staff on the direction and changes you want to make.

- Develop ad hoc committees *at all levels* to champion the cultural change.

- Begin to communicate, first to supervisors, then to all employees, why the company is evolving and how that evolution will affect individuals.

- Establish two-way communication channels with employees to get feedback, communicate adjustments, and measure attitudes.

- Set clear objectives and milestones, preferably tied to specific timelines and compensation.

- Create ongoing weekly activities that are directly related to overall objectives and milestones.

- Establish benchmarks, measure progress, and communicate results.

- Reward achievement and celebrate success.

- Be consistent.

- Be patient.

From Commodities to Solutions

Cargill, Inc., a large, privately held company in the United States, had, in its fiscal year ending in 2005, revenues of $71 billion and 105,000 employees in fifty-nine countries. From humble beginnings operating a single grain elevator in 1865, Cargill built a formidable, global commodities trading organization. Originating grains and supplying agricultural products such as flour, oils, and corn products to food processors had been Cargill's core business for more than 135 years. By the late 1990s, the food industry was rapidly changing. Cargill's customers in the retail food industry were consolidating and seeking new products and services from Cargill.

Their customers—consumers—were demanding a greater variety of prepackaged, easy to prepare products.

Strategic Intent   Cargill's market position appeared to be stagnating, and that prompted senior management to rethink its business strategy. The company began the journey of changing away from a commodity mindset and a shift in its business from basic commodities into one that produced higher-value products and services through research, innovation, and collaboration with its customers.

In 1999, Cargill's senior management developed a decade-long plan they called "Strategic Intent" with the following mission:

> By the year 2010, Cargill will be the recognized global leader in providing agrifood chain customers with solutions to enable them to succeed in their businesses.

Cargill defined a "customer solution" as an integrated combination of products and services that solve a problem or create unique opportunities for the customer.

Leading the Cultural Revolution   To achieve this monumental shift for the company, Cargill started with a Corporate Leadership Team of senior executives who worked together to change Cargill's business and culture. This team began by mapping out elements necessary to become a solutions company. Employees across the company were asked to participate in a worldwide culture scan to identify cultural artifacts, including letters, activities, beliefs, behaviors, signage, objects, and stories that collectively helped to define Cargill's corporate culture. Then the company's leaders participated in a Global Forum to determine which artifacts should be incorporated into the new culture and which should be thrown out. This exercise and the definition of the old Cargill culture produced a visceral response from managers and helped clarify the essential new Cargill culture. In addition, an annual companywide employee engagement survey was instituted to measure employees' involvement, commitment, and satisfaction worldwide. This survey, combined with a 360-degree feedback exercise in which managers were evaluated by supervisors, peers, and direct reports, provided the insights necessary to continuously improve each manager's performance.

The strategic intent team also identified six behaviors critical to the success of strategic intent, and they were incorporated into all employees' annual performance reviews:

1. Discuss, Decide, Support

2. Respect, Candor, Commitment

3. Challenge, Change, Innovate

4. Ensure and Accept Accountability

5. Pursue and Reinforce Collaboration

6. Develop Deep Customer Knowledge and Insights

To ensure that transforming cultural change continues, Cargill has introduced a variety of ongoing cultural and communication activities, such as global town hall meetings in which managers can participate in a conference call to hear directly from senior management about issues and challenges, new initiatives, financial results, and other significant corporate news. The centerpiece of these town meetings is the success stories of business units that have developed and delivered new customer solutions.

In addition to cultural activities, Cargill has made significant investments in research and development, equipment, marketing, and training to ensure that the company has the talent and resources necessary for change. As part of its strategic intent, Cargill recognized that changing its culture from a commodities company to a solutions company would take ten years, and that the journey would be ongoing. Therefore, development of the leadership and management talent and skills for the new solutions company and culture is a continuous effort.

Stable leadership has been a hallmark of Cargill's management development philosophy. Jim Haymaker, Corporate Vice President of Strategy and Business Development for Cargill, states, "We have realized that the successful implementation of a corporate strategy is more dependent on shaping culture and management discipline than simply restructuring business processes." To this end, Cargill is dedicated to building true customer partnerships based on culture, values, and solutions.[1]

The Corporate Leadership Team documented the steps necessary to consistently replicate the journey from running a commodities business to creating a customer solutions enterprise. The Cargill businesses use this template to conduct their own individual transformations. A comprehensive series of Customer Solutions booklets were designed as training and reference tools for all business unit managers. Each is motivated by incentives based on implementation and performance.

Creating Partners   The new Customer Solutions system contained a number of significant insights. Cargill concluded that trust was the linchpin for building collaborative, solutions-driven relationships with customers. Their relationship goals are to build customer loyalty through shared innovation, shared risk, and shared value creation, resulting in tight organizational partnerships. These long-term relationships will result in increased profits and a competitive advantage for Cargill's customers and thus for Cargill itself.

Another key insight focused on prospective customer selection. Cargill came to understand that traditional market segmentation would not ensure successful relationships. As a result, the company established a rigorous evaluation process of its current customers and prospects based on strategic readiness. *Strategic readiness* was defined as a customer's readiness for solutions and ability to cross-integrate systems and innovations. Willingness to share information—including financial information—and enter into joint working teams and alliances was deemed critical.

Beyond shared processes, Cargill has learned that trust, collaboration, and innovation are the corporate values and behaviors that need to be in alignment with customers in order to achieve lasting, authentic partnerships.

Results   Five years of increased employee engagement, combined with a relentless commitment to cultural transformation, has resulted in new customer solutions and remarkable growth. Cargill's revenue has increased from $49 billion in 2001 to $71 billion in 2005. Earnings have jumped from $333 million to $1.5 billion. Their focus on customer solutions continues to reshape the culture of Cargill.

What Happened to Quality?

In the 1980s, many companies made quality the centerpiece of their businesses. There were quality circles, quality initiatives, and intensive quality training. Everyone read the latest quality book and hired quality gurus to help transform their companies.

After the initial employee kickoff meeting, things looked like they were really on track. But many companies found that they couldn't sustain the quality program beyond the first phase. People either didn't know how to integrate the training to their jobs or were resistant to change. Some companies abandoned their quality programs before they ever got off the ground. A lack of long-range planning and employee buy-in killed many quality programs.

Getting Senior Management Buy-In

As is true with most major initiatives, the possibility of success is remote without buy-in from senior management. Understanding and supporting Balanced Culture must begin with the CEO and senior staff. First, there must be agreement that alignment between corporate values and stakeholder values is imperative to the organization's long-term success. Senior managers must become personally involved in the early stages of developing a strategic plan for cultural evolution and change. It is their responsibility to help create and articulate the vision for internal change. They are also accountable to all stakeholders for explaining and defending the company's actions. Because the goal of Balanced Culture is to stay in alignment with stakeholder values, these actions are usually met with positive external support.

In Howard Gardner's book *Changing Minds*,[2] the author explores how creating convincing narratives can help people and organizations change direction. Using a variety of examples from business, academia, and government, Gardner provides fascinating insights on how people change their minds. He has developed what he calls the "seven key levers for changing minds": reason, research, resonance, representational redescriptions, resources/rewards, real-world events, and resistances. Gardner warns about leaders using rhetoric that does not reflect the real world. A hyperbolic narrative cannot be sustained over time. (However, Margaret Thatcher, Ronald Reagan, and Jack Welch are all examples of gifted leaders who created compelling narratives that ultimately changed people's minds.) Gardner shows us how the forces of education, narratives, arts, and science often shape and influence our perceptions. *Changing Minds* identifies the most important elements present in changing everything from vast populations to individual relationships.

[If you want to drive change in your organization, start with a compelling narrative.]

A Manifesto for Change

Most corporations inevitably face a crossroads where a profound shift in their culture or the way they do business is needed to achieve alignment. A manifesto is a valuable tool for clearly stating your company's intentions while soliciting support for the actions stated in the manifesto. The word *manifesto* is defined as "a public declaration of intentions or principles." It is a galvanizing document that is the catalyst for all corporate change.

Creating a manifesto often helps the company clarify its vision. If done with a persuasive narrative that is actionable throughout the organization, the manifesto becomes a call to action. It spells out the strategic intent for all to see. By its nature, a manifesto also requires a stated commitment from all participants. That's why the manifesto known as the Declaration of Independence was signed by its authors and defenders. Developing a persuasive manifesto is a powerful instrument for inciting cultural change.

Getting Everyone on Board

After establishing a clear vision, senior management support, and a manifesto for change, it's time to get everyone on board. As stated earlier, many people abhor change. The fear of loss or the uncertainty of the future creates a powerful resistance to change. Employees look to supervisors, managers, and executives to gauge commitment to the new vision.

The evolution narrative must be convincing enough to overcome initial fears by creating a clear path to a better future. While it may be easy to see the importance of all stakeholder values at the senior management level, it may be more difficult for front-line employees to see the big picture. The explanation and rationale for the manifesto must present the broad view in its introduction, while being clear on the implications for each employee. You must answer the most pressing employee questions: "How will this affect me?" "What do you want me to do?" "And why should I care?"

This can be accomplished by having all managers meet with individual employees to explain how the manifesto impacts their department and jobs. It is also an opportunity to get direct feedback from employees on their anxieties, frustrations, and fears. The empowerment that comes from the feeling of being heard is a crucial step in ensuring support for change. However, many companies solicit feedback and then do nothing with it, which is more destructive than not soliciting feedback at all.

It's critically important not only to listen to employees' concerns but to quickly and directly respond to those concerns, even if it's only to acknowledge that you can't fix the problem right now. This is a chance for management to clearly demonstrate that they intend to get it right.

We have used our work with Lawson as an example throughout Chapters Seven and Eight to illustrate the BalancedBrand concepts of a manifesto and core narrative. By reading about the steps that Lawson went through in 2004 and 2005, you will be able to see how The BalancedBrand System helped Lawson navigate its cultural and market changes by creating values alignment.

Lawson's Time for Change

Lawson Software was a $350 million business specializing in enterprise system business applications. Established in 1975, Lawson was a privately held, family-run organization that prided itself on software applications that were built to meet the specific needs of its customers and responsive customer service. During the 1990s, Lawson watched as its competitors—Oracle, PeopleSoft, and SAP—eclipsed it in the marketplace. While Lawson had experienced significant success in developing enterprise software systems for the health care industry, it missed the growth occurring in most other sectors of the economy.

In 2001, Lawson completed its long-anticipated initial public offering (IPO). Within the company, there was mounting excitement that once Lawson went public it would be perceived as finally having made "the big time." However, shortly after the IPO was completed, the internal reaction was disappointment. In hindsight, the timing of the IPO couldn't have been worse. With the economy in the technology sector tanking, Lawson found itself faced with rapidly declining share price and lower-than-expected sales and revenue.

Significant layoffs happened for the first time in the company's history, and senior management spent the next two years firefighting in order to keep the company strong through the downturn. As a result of all the turmoil, employee morale was very low.

In 2004, Lawson began realigning its corporate values using The BalancedBrand System. In addition to their work on values alignment, senior management at Lawson began actively looking for a merger opportunity that would give the combined organizations global reach with a complete set of enterprise system business applications to compete in the midmarket. These efforts resulted in a merger in 2005 between Lawson and Intentia, a Swedish enterprise software company with complementary values, products, and services. As part of the merger, Harry Debes was named president and CEO of Lawson. Debes immediately set about creating a "performance culture" that simplified compensation plans to focus on cost containment and revenue growth. He conveyed to all managers that "this was a team sport; we win or lose together—so everyone must help everyone else all the time." The management team set specific short-term financial goals and then monitored everyone's weekly performance toward the achievement of those goals.

Lawson in the United States, and Intentia in Sweden, had been working on parallel tracks of delivering world-class software and service solutions to their discrete client base. Both companies had built strong reputations for innovation, collaboration, and service. However, neither company had the resources to offer a full suite of enterprise business process solutions for the global midmarket.

Lawson's focus is service sector categories such as health care, government, education, retail, and financial services, while Intentia's industry-specific focus is apparel, food and beverage, wholesale, asset intensive, and manufacturing. As single entities, both companies were struggling to compete with Oracle and SAP. However, the combined companies shared a strong heritage in serving midmarket customers that had been ignored by the big players until recently. The battle for the emerging midmarket had just begun. Analysts agree that during the next decade most of the growth in enterprise software will come from the midmarket segment.

Lawson's Manifesto

In 2004, *time* was the centerpiece of Lawson's Manifesto.[3] The document articulated how the company would use time as a currency to differentiate itself in the marketplace:

- More time spent with customers
- Less time in the implementation of software programs
- Respecting customers' time through service, product quality, and efficacy

Lawson's Manifesto Copy

We believe it's time for a change in the business applications industry.
The market is insisting on it.
And software companies ignore that insistence at their peril.
The insistence is rooted in dissatisfaction.
A minority of users would recommend their incumbent provider to others.
In this landscape, there is enormous opportunity.
We are seizing this opportunity.
Going forward, this is our vision. Breaking away.
We will break away from the competition by setting industry-wide change in motion, acting on these convictions.
It's time a software company put client interests squarely, convincingly and unmistakably first.
It's time that business applications fulfilled their promises of improved control, efficiency, productivity and bottom-line benefits.
It's time for the demo to be the reality of the user's experience, and for the "upgrade" to mean measurable improvement in that experience.
The change we will set in motion is, itself, about time.

It's about delivering information technology that gives clients time to focus on what is important to them, in their jobs and in their lives.

It's about deploying information technology to find time for clients—time that helps them keep pace with a world that is always speeding up—time that helps them move more quickly.

It's about respecting clients' time—investing our time to understand their challenges and bring them solutions specific to their needs.

It's about accelerating clients' time to realization of measurable value. It's about saving clients time when they are live on our applications. It's about maximizing time returned to clients by helping them extend our applications to widespread strategic use.

It's about fulfilling a compelling promise.

Lawson delivers software and services that put time on your side.

In 2005, the new management team at Lawson evaluated the Manifesto to determine which parts of the document would be relevant to the new "performance culture." They were concerned because the organization had lost focus in delivering the Manifesto promises as a result of management's attention being diverted to the merger with Intentia. In the fall of 2005, senior managers began refocusing with customer input on the Manifesto to deliver on the promises that are important to the marketplace. The Manifesto continues to be one dimension for creating Lawson's Balanced Culture. It provides an important lens to evaluate customer service.

Telling the World

Once the strategy is in place and your company is actively making changes to align corporate values with stakeholder values, it's time to make a public declaration of intent. In this phase of change, explaining your manifesto to all stakeholders is crucial to gaining acceptance and support in the marketplace. It's impossible to create perfect alignment with all stakeholders because of differing values and agendas. But the level of clarity with which your company states its case and the potential impact on stakeholders has direct influence on the outcome. The narrative you create for public consumption must be based in real-world experience. Overpromising or falling back on vague rhetoric damages your credibility and reputation.

Don't expect everyone to be thrilled with your choices. While they may not completely agree with your direction, most stakeholders will respect your commitment and focus. Initial feedback will provide valuable information for calibrating future actions.

Here's the good news: Because Balanced Culture is an ongoing activity, you don't have to do everything at once. Often, stakeholders will support your direction if they understand that you will be addressing their concerns at some future date. Managing stakeholder expectations is a crucial element in creating and maintaining balance.

Balanced Culture is a way for a company to connect two important factors:

1. What do we do as a company?
2. What do our stakeholders want?

Often, just asking those two questions can lead to major change in an organization. That is exactly what launched Microsoft's amazing turn toward a Web-based environment.

Turning on a Dime: Microsoft Moves to the Web

It may now seem a faint memory, but Microsoft once believed that it was in the operating system development business. Evidence certainly pointed in that direction—all those $89 copies of Windows on personal computers had led the company to $6 billion in sales by 1995. But customers began to want something different from their computing life—creating documents wasn't enough, and now they wanted to share more, learn more, connect more. Until the mid-1990s, Microsoft had a reputation of being insular in their product and market development. While they were totally focused on creating a new version of Windows, the rest of the technology world was rapidly moving toward Internet access tools.

Shifting Markets and Values   While visiting his alma mater, a Microsoft executive made a startling discovery.[4] In an urgent memo to leadership, he warned that college campuses were more wired, in many cases, than most corporations. This discovery caused Microsoft to realize that they were in jeopardy of not being a significant player in the rapidly growing Internet business. Microsoft's leaders reassessed the significance of the rise of Netscape, America Online, Java, and the World Wide Web itself. They asked the questions, "What business are we in, and what do our customers want?" and they got different answers than even a few years earlier.

On December 7, 1995, Bill Gates gave perhaps the most significant speech of his career, letting his own employees and the rest of the world know that Microsoft was going to have to move fast to stay in balance. On the anniversary of the Pearl Harbor attack, he quoted Japanese Admiral Yamamoto, saying, "I fear we have awakened a sleeping giant." He assigned Internet compatibility the highest level of importance within the organization, and launched an intensive effort to ensure that every member of the company understood what needed to happen next.

Changing Microsoft to a Web-focused strategy entailed redirecting nearly 20,000 workers. It was a Herculean challenge. The advantage of having a focused and driven leader is that the direction can be clear, and resources can be shifted. By August 1996, Microsoft had unveiled Explorer 3.0, a Web-browsing software.[5]

Aligning with the marketplace is the key to survival in today's marketplace. In Microsoft's case, management understood that they could no longer rely solely on their customers' legacy operating systems business to provide future growth. Once corporate values realigned with customers' values, the company was able to create significant internal change to meet new goals.

Unifying Customer Experience

It's difficult to transform a culture without a clear picture of what you want to be. The Unifying Customer Experience draws that picture. As an exercise to understand the Unifying Customer Experience, ask your senior managers to write, in the customers' words, what it would be like to work with your company and to use your products or services 1,000 days from today.

The resulting narrative will provide a framework for changes and actions your organization needs to implement in order to succeed. By asking the following questions, you can build a Unifying Customer Experience:

- What do we want our customers to say about our products and services in 1,000 days?
- What changes do we have to make in order for our customers to have the experience they desire?
- What specific changes will be made in the areas of aspiration, process, and impact to align with stakeholder values?
- How will these changes affect my department, team, and personal performance?
- Who will be responsible for ensuring that these changes will occur?
- How will we measure our customers' experiences throughout our change process?
- What will we do with the feedback from employees and customers?

A good start to this exercise is the creation of a Unifying Customer Experience workbook that can be shared with all employees. In that workbook, each employee is asked to help set department, team, and individual goals, and then commit to completing the goals in a certain timeframe. The workbook can be used as part of an incentive and/or recognition program. In combination with the manifesto, the Unifying Customer Experience book creates two effective management tools for aligning corporate values with stakeholder values.

Lawson's Unifying Customer Experience

A key tool in helping Lawson employees understand the Manifesto was to create a Unifying Customer Experience book called the *Manifesto in Action*.[6] This book described, in the voice of the customer, what it would be like to do business with Lawson at the end of 1,000 days. Everything from improved customer service to time-finding product performance was outlined in the *Manifesto in Action*. The book was used to help employees understand what they needed to do to help customers have the experience promised. The book personalized the cultural changes the company needed to implement in order to deliver the time vision. Each employee was asked to sign a commitment to the *Manifesto in Action*, and it was used as a training tool and a discussion guide for managers and employees.

Excerpts from Lawson's *Manifesto in Action*

A Client's Story 2007

Lawson a Great Brand

> When I realized my organization had a problem, my first thoughts were to go to a company that had a reputation for solving problems like mine.
>
> Lawson was at the top of the list. It seems they are behind every success story in my industry.
>
> I heard Lawson is a different kind of solutions company. They are known for keeping their promises and solving critical business issues for people like me. . . .
>
> Ultimately, I knew that in working with Lawson, I could learn from their experts even during the buying process. They promised me they could

help me solve my problems while freeing up my time to focus on other priorities. And it was clear that they walked their talk. From the beginning, each Lawson team member clearly sacrificed their time before they asked me to sacrifice mine. . . .

Lawson a Great Choice

One expectation I had for our selection committee was that we visit their corporate headquarters and experience the "Proof of Concept" Lab. Here, they showed me how their unique blend of software, technology services, and organizational consulting would solve my problems. . . .

Lawson didn't talk about individual products. They focused on the total solution. . . . Perhaps the greatest difference between Lawson and others in the industry was the fact that Lawson helped us understand that our goals and their goals were one and the same. In other words, a true partnership. They were willing to put their money where their mouth was. . . .

Lawson a Great Value

By the time I was ready to make a commitment to Lawson, it was obvious they had saved me time. I didn't have to sell their solutions internally, because they had already earned the vote of my steering committee. . . .

Lawson a Great Experience

Lawson continued to show their unique approach when the same team that consulted with me prior to the contract signing was back on-site ready to begin the project. Lawson called this continuity of care, eliminating wasted time that inevitably occurs when projects are handed off from one team to the next.

I was literally shocked at how quickly Lawson had the software installed and running on my site. My team was able to see the software, and immediately get excited for the completion of the project. This first impression was important to kick off the change management process which Lawson led us through from beginning to end.

Manifesto in Action was used to help employees understand what they needed to do to help customers have the experience promised.

The book personalized the changes the company needed to implement in order to deliver their vision. Each employee was asked to sign a commitment to the *Manifesto in Action*, and it was used as a training tool and a discussion guide for managers and employees.

1,000/100-Day Plan

Like the quality programs we discussed earlier, it is imperative to write a plan that creates a vision for the long term, while being actionable in the short term. The 1,000-Day Plan is a high-ideal method for setting achievable long-term goals. The 1,000-Day Plan helps the whole organization understand what your business or service will look like in the future. By breaking the 1,000-Day Plan into smaller 100-Day segments, it is easy to create short-term goals that will keep the whole organization involved and focused.

One key to success is to keep it simple. Write only two or three 100-Day Plans at a time. This provides enough continuity for managers and employees to understand what needs to be done without getting too far out ahead of reality. The 100-Day Plan should be reviewed four to five times during that period, as a way to stay on track.

Milestones, Incentives, and Recognition

In addition to the 1,000-Day Plan, it's important to recognize and celebrate key milestones. All employees must see how organizational changes have the potential to positively impact their compensation and careers. Using incentives and recognition to motivate and change performance is critical to the success of building Balanced Culture. Without reinforcement, the organization will begin to resent and ultimately reject changes. Incentives should be used to help achieve short-term goals.

Recognition is most effective when used to reward overall performance.

Recognition programs that become a long-standing tradition grow in power exponentially as they are repeated each year. Studies have found that recognition can be more powerful than money. However, recognition loses support when people are not adequately compensated for doing outstanding work. So using recognition and incentives together creates the optimal performance tools.

Balance in Motion

Motion is the essence of a BalancedBrand. Organizations must continuously measure, correct, respond, evolve, and grow in order to thrive. Maintaining balance is about building those actions into all operating systems of your organization.

Companies that have embraced a culture of change that can quickly adjust to dynamic environments are the most formidable businesses in the world. Balanced Culture is a process, not an event. Like any new skill, your company will feel awkward at first when trying to achieve it. However, over the next 1,000 days, Balanced Culture will become second nature to your organization, and the difference will be noticeable.

Balance is maintained when you're willing to stay in motion. It relies upon the ability to recognize when corrections are needed, while neither over- or undercompensating for the forces influencing your company. Business is dynamic. There are variable speeds at which business cycles, Wall Street demands, and customer preferences are all changing. But while the fact of change is inevitable, building a corporate culture that readily adapts to change is well worth the effort.

[Motion is essential to creating balance.

Business is dynamic.]

The one piece most organizations tend to let slide is a commitment to values monitoring. You need ongoing feedback on how your stakeholders' values are changing. By simply listening and responding to stakeholders through systematic research and established listening posts, you'll have the information necessary to create a competitive advantage. This is a proven way to build and protect a strong brand and reputation.

Conflicting Values

It is common to find stakeholder values that are at odds with the majority of other stakeholder values. Close examination of these conflicting values presents great opportunities or threats to an organization, brand, or reputation. By identifying and monitoring the entire range of stakeholder values, it's possible to find ways to achieve alignment and a Balanced Culture.

Identifying Imbalance

There is an alarming erosion of investor, customer, and community confidence in business. The most recent Reputation Institute studies have shown that no American company scored higher than 79 points out of 100.[7] Organizations find it increasingly difficult to reverse the erosion of confidence in a rapidly changing global economy.

By using the Factiva Insight monitoring system, your company will have a clear reading on which corporate values and stakeholder values are out of alignment. These potential Flashpoints form the starting points for change. Developing the appropriate corrective actions and implementing those actions companywide is the first step in creating Balanced Culture.

Chapter Seven Summary

Balanced Culture

The purpose of Balanced Culture is to help the organization embrace the power of alignment of corporate values with stakeholder values.

Change Versus Evolution

Movement and evolution are essential for Balanced Culture, but many employees will resist change at first.

Guidelines for Balanced Culture

- Ensure that you have a clear picture of your current corporate culture.
- Prepare an in-depth review of how well your corporate culture aligns with stakeholder-assigned values.
- Review your corporate vision and operating values to identify possible gaps between your organization and your stakeholders' values.
- Get buy-in from senior staff on the direction and changes you want to make.
- Develop ad hoc committees at all levels to champion the cultural change.
- Keep up two-way communications on why the company is evolving and how that evolution will affect each individual employee.
- Institute clear objectives and milestones, preferably tied to specific timelines and compensation.

Manifesto

An organization's public intent for change. Culture change should begin with a manifesto, or public declaration of intentions or principles.

Unifying Customer Experience
The Unifying Customer Experience outlines what an organization would like its customers to say about it in 1,000 days. This document creates a vision that each employee can use to plan how they will impact the customer experience.

1,000/100-Day Plan
Prepare a 1,000/100-Day Plan to create a vision for the long term and remain actionable in the short term.

Milestones, Incentives, and Recognition
- Create sustaining weekly activities that are directly related to overall objectives and milestones.
- Reward achievement and celebrate success.
- Be consistent.
- Be patient.

Balance in Motion
Motion is essential to creating balance. Business is dynamic.

Balanced Conversation

balancedconversation

If You Want to Build a
Relationship, Start a Conversation

Words . . .

Have the power to create or destroy
relationships.

Lasting relationships start with a conversation.

> *"launching campaigns"*   **"closing the sale"**
>
> **"demand creation"**   "re-upping the customer"
>
> **"compelling arguments"**   "making the numbers"
>
> "market penetration"   *"sell and repent"*

Sound familiar? This is how most businesspeople sound when they talk about sales and marketing. There is nothing in this language that would even hint at the possibility of a relationship. Yet, for all this wall-building talk, companies continue to claim that building relationships with their customers is their most important goal.

Language shapes attitudes and actions. Think about how customer conversations influence untold aspects of your business. A real conversation requires common interests, discussion, listening, and respect for one another's point of view. Most relationships are built upon ongoing conversations.

Balanced Conversation

There are two ways to have a Balanced Conversation. First and most obvious is by talking directly to your stakeholders. This is achieved through all stakeholder contact with your company. The second way to create a conversation is by having others talk about your company. This occurs when people discuss personal experiences with your company, see media coverage or advertising. In all cases, these conversations are opportunities to build your brand and reputation.

[
Balanced Conversation identifies all the possible points of contact with key stakeholders in which communications can initiate, reinforce, and strengthen relationships.
]

Anyone Home?

What might happen if we used common business language in our personal lives?

A car pulls into the driveway of a suburban bungalow, and a woman, lugging a briefcase and an armful of dry cleaning, trudges up the walk. As she enters the house, her husband comes to the door, putting out his arms for a hug. She avoids his embrace and sticks out her hand for a firm handshake, saying, "Bob, I'm pleased to be back home, and I'm excited about the opportunity to share my ideas for future family efficiency in the coming fiscal year."

The man, still stuck in her handshake grip, asks with alarm, "Honey, do you feel all right?"

"I'm fine," she says with a smile in her voice. "I have prepared a thirty-minute PowerPoint presentation with fifteen minutes for Q&A that I want to review with you and your colleagues, er, our children, during dinner. But don't worry about taking notes," she adds, grinning, "because I brought color handouts for everyone." The man shrinks back in alarm.

"Mom, is that you?" ask two small voices, as the children enter the room.

"Lauren and Benjamin, so glad to see you two again," says Mom, shaking hands.

"We just saw you this morning," say the confused children.

Mom replies, "Strong relationships require frequent contact. Our ability to spend down time together not only builds trust, but will take our relationship to the next level!"

As ridiculous as it is to imagine using stilted business language in a family setting, think for a moment about the way your organization interacts with customers and other stakeholders. The conversation presented illustrates that there is nothing natural or even remotely human in many "business discussions" that are bandied about the office. We may not be pleased to present our ideas. We may not wish to have frequent contact and conversations. Often, we bludgeon our listeners with the same tired ideas, and we fail to hear their input.

If you have genuine conversations with your customer, you may learn some worthwhile information, such as who is having a problem, who wants to spend more time with you, who was disappointed by a product or service recently. Relationships can't grow or thrive without conversations, yet most of us make all our business interactions like those in the example, with lots of carefully crafted language and no room for input.

Sales Versus Relationships

With most customer conversations, the initial contact is typically a salesperson whose orientation will be either to make the sale or to create a relationship. In a sales-oriented process, the salesperson is trying to highlight features and benefits, overcome objections, and close the sale. In a relationship-oriented process, the salesperson is trying to identify the needs of the customer, listen to concerns, and ultimately find a solution that fits the customer's needs—with the sale being secondary to solving the customer's problem. But the conversation doesn't end there. Relationship-driven companies continuously look for ways to stay in contact with their customers and become trusted advisers. These are the relationships that are difficult, if not impossible, for the competition to break.

Focusing on sales versus relationships has to do with how much time you want to spend with the customer and how important a long-term relationship is to the company. It's true that the quicker you close sales, the more sales you can make. But a few more moments with the customer may lead to more sales. Understanding the lifetime value of the customer plays a crucial role in corporate decisions to build relationships.

Campaign-Based Marketing	*Conversation-Based Marketing*
Launch a campaign	Initiate a conversation
Make a compelling argument	Find common ground
Market penetration	Relationship building
Demand creation	Values alignment
Re-up the customer	Extend the relationship
Sales driven	Relationship oriented
Leverage the relationship	Mutual interests
Customer-centric	Relationship-centric

A cohesive conversation requires that everyone in the company have a clear idea about the content. Internal conversations are necessary to help people understand the vision, values, and core narrative. Getting employees' feedback is the first step in building a single corporate voice. Most employees will not enter into a conversation with the customer or stakeholders without first feeling comfortable with the subject.

[
Creating meaningful conversations, centered on customer needs, is still the best way to build relationships.
]

Creating a Conversation

Alex Bogusky, Creative Director of Crispen Porter + Bogusky, redefined advertising based on initiating and sustaining conversations. Through reframing advertising from campaign-based to conversation-based, the agency's work took on a whole new dimension. Their award-winning work for MINI Cooper and IKEA are examples of compelling conversations, not advertising campaigns.

In the MINI Cooper conversations, they introduced the idea of the "art of motoring," which embodies the whole philosophy of the company, product, and drivers. MINI Cooper owners are portrayed as being friendly, individualistic enthusiasts who have a love and appreciation for well-designed compact cars. The agency doesn't think in terms of advertising, public relations, and promotions, but rather in terms of developing "creative content" for the ongoing conversation. This philosophy opened the door to building unique nontraditional media, such as putting a new MINI Cooper in an airport on a stand that resembled a children's ride.[1]

These groundbreaking ideas advanced the MINI Cooper philosophy and brand personality while garnering significant public relations attention at a modest cost. By describing all advertising and public relations as "creative content," Bogusky blurred the line between the two disciplines. The fluidity of the conversation is present in the tone and scope of the communications. In addition, Bogusky calls media planning and placement "content delivery," once again expanding the traditional role of the media department in an advertising agency. These subtle changes in language create a whole new approach to marketing and communications. By aspiring to create a conversation, the agency team takes a greater responsibility in building lasting customer relationships.

While Bogusky has begun changing the advertising industry, much work needs to be done in extending the philosophy of conversations to public relations and corporate communications. We believe this can be achieved through a concept called "Core Narrative."

Stories

For tens of thousands of years, humans have taught each generation the history of important events, social mores, and traditions by using hieroglyphics, parables, oral histories, and storytelling. The role of the storyteller, shaman, priest, rabbi, or cleric is to help create narratives that are relevant in shaping people's values, lives, and actions. Which is easier to remember, details of a PowerPoint presentation or a powerful story?

Balanced Conversation relies on our ability to create meaningful dialogues that get customers' attention by being relevant and valuable, not repetitive and intrusive. That doesn't mean we can't be compelling, entertaining, and charming. Great storytellers and conversationalists are always interesting and engaging. They know when to listen, when to change the subject, and how to keep the conversation moving.

In many ways advertising, public relations, and sales executives are the modern equivalent of business storytellers and conversationalists. However, the practice of advertising and public relations too often stalls out in messaging rather than telling the story. Messaging is simply a set of ideas that demonstrate a point of view. It is less inviting and insightful than a good story, and it is much less likely to result in a relationship.

Core Narrative Model

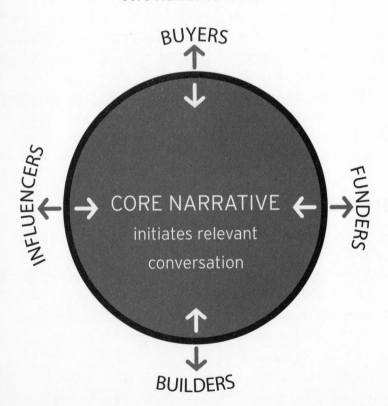

Core Narrative

What is the most relevant story to tell each stakeholder group? When we meet someone for the first time, we don't automatically tell our life story the same way each time. We make decisions about what part of our story, if any, is appropriate to tell. We also take a point in time in which to begin our story. Imagine what it would be like if everyone you met told you their life story starting at birth. Businesses do this all the time. Who cares that your bank is 100 years old, or who needs to know the name of the founder? However, customers do care about security and new product or service offerings. Once we get to know someone, we may pick up the story at the point that is most relevant to our audience. What's more, we understand that our story is more interesting if we involve the audience. In this way, the story is not just about us but reflects shared experiences or values.

Imagine hearing renowned documentary filmmaker Ken Burns tell your business story as a miniseries. What would your company's story be? Who is the audience? What would they find relevant? How would the story end?

To create your unique business story the Core Narrative must consider the following elements:

- *Basic History:* A timeline of major milestones that provide rudimentary facts about your business
- *Vision:* A basic premise explaining why you are in business and clearly delineates where you are going
- *Characters:* Relevant background on people, products, and services that play a central role in the company's history, values, and personality
- *Pinnacle Events:* The pivotal events, decisions, and activities that defined the course of the company
- *Side Stories:* Individual anecdotes created for a specific audience that demonstrate mutual values such as commitment to service, dedication to quality, and remarkable business practices

- *Conclusion:* What it all means to the audience and why they should care

This becomes the Core Narrative from which all communications flow. Advertising, public relations, product literature, and internal communications must have a viable connection to the Core Narrative. Without these connect points, your story can easily become disjointed and irrelevant.

Completing Each Other: The Lawson Story Continues

In 2005, Lawson and Intentia announced their merger as one of equals. The combined companies generated revenue of more than $900 million serving 6,000 clients in 40 countries. Unlike most mergers that tend to be either hostile takeovers or shotgun weddings, Lawson and Intentia shared similar values and complementary software applications. Both companies agreed to retain the Lawson name going forward. Using the complementary strengths of both companies, Lawson has a realistic chance of dominating the midmarket. Their existing customer base is made up of primarily midmarket clients. So they have the advantage of having built software applications and services to the right fit for this market. Midmarket customers know they can get software, global service, and scalability without having to compromise.

Lawson Core Narrative

The following is the revised Core Narrative that explains why Lawson Software and Intentia joined forces to become the "new" Lawson.[2]

> *They were:*
> *Two companies that shared the same vision and values.*
> *Two companies that served and collaborated with aspiring global customers.*

Two companies whose technologies and services completed each other.
   They shared:
One goal . . . to be the global leader in serving the midmarket with world-class enterprise software applications and solutions.
   Aspiring companies were forced to use enterprise business process solutions that were either too big or too small. Large ERP providers offered stability and scalability but with products and services that catered to mammoth customers. Small ERP providers lacked the stability, scalability and global service to adequately serve the midmarket.
   Lawson is just right.
   It was the right time to move . . . boldly beyond the competition . . . together with our clients, our partners and each other.
   And because Lawson offers the size, stability and services tailored to the midmarket . . .

Lawson's Core Narrative is used for all communications to ensure a single voice in messages related to brand, reputation, positioning, and brand personality.

Results

The overall results of these changes will not be known for some time; however, Lawson has already gained significant attention in the marketplace. Analysts and the press have confirmed that Lawson is a leading player in the midmarket category of enterprise software. At the 2005 CUE event, an analyst told Lawson executives that he'd been skeptical of the Manifesto and Lawson's service promises, but now believes that the company's actions were industry changing. The enterprise software industry has responded by introducing its own manifestos and customer service programs.

Lawson customers have reacted with great enthusiasm and support for Lawson's commitment to change. Employees have reported that the new direction has provided clarity and a strong mandate for action. These are all very positive indicators that Lawson is on the right track toward a BalancedBrand.

Stakeholder Points of Contact

Every point of contact is an opportunity to create, strengthen, or destroy a relationship. By methodically identifying all possible contact points, you can strategically use the whole array of marketing tools to create relationships. When the tools start relevant conversations, your customers might actually put down the in-flight magazine and visit with you for a while.

There are two techniques for mapping out points of contact.

Using the Value Dimensions of Aspiration, Process, and Impact, it is easy to chart all possible points of contact. When you understand how to reach a key stakeholder, the challenge becomes finding new and innovative ways to start a conversation.

Determining Points of Contact

- Advertising
- Internet
- Web Site
- Direct Mail
- Brochures
- Media
- Word of Mouth
- Other
- Users

ASPIRATION

BUYERS POINTS OF CONTACT/ VALUES

PROCESS

- Purchase Experience
- Product Performance
- Service Experience
- Direct Contact with the Company
- Repair/Warranty Work
- Customer Service

IMPACT

- Media
- Associations
- Public Service
- Community Activities

Initiating a Conversation

Advertising and public relations professionals can start a conversation with stakeholders if the creative content is designed with that goal in mind. Often, companies view the message as a self-contained creative unit. Instead, think of it as an opportunity to create a more in-depth dialogue with stakeholders. When you take this approach, and align the narrative with stakeholder values, you are both memorable and compelling. This is an excellent way to begin a conversation.

Sustaining a Conversation

Sustaining the conversation requires reciprocity. If a conversation is interesting, we want to participate, and most important, we want to be heard. There's no such thing as too much listening, and everyone can do a better job at it.

The most important element of a conversation is the ability to listen *and* to respond. One-way communications are not conversations; they're monologues. From a marketing perspective, a real conversation is two-way; it is responsive and respectful to the customer. The goal of this level of communication is to build lasting relationships. All relationships start with conversations.

It is easier to talk than to listen. The same is true for companies. We are so focused on getting our message out that we don't invest the time, money, or resources to get input. Investors and directors get our ear. Unfortunately, others, such as employees and the community, may have a harder time getting through.

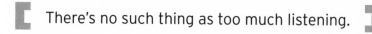

There's no such thing as too much listening.

Technology has made it easier for many stakeholders to participate in the conversation. Through the Internet, we can create ongoing dialogue with stakeholders around the world by simply using

Web chats, user groups, e-mails, and blogs. The Web has enabled diverse groups to come together and build stronger relationships.

Keep the Message, Change the Inflection

All stakeholders have their own values, so it will be impossible to have the same conversation with every group. While the subject may be the same, the nuances of what's important and how to conduct a conversation differ with each group. Just as we don't speak to our families or spouses the same way we speak to a coworker, we also don't speak to customers the same way that we speak to analysts or shareholders. Creating conversations using BalancedBrand tools will help you engage each stakeholder group in the future success of your company.

[
The personalized conversation:
Same topic + different person = new inflection.
]

Before you start a conversation, you must know your audience, what's important to them and how they would like to be addressed. Building separate strategies for each stakeholder group is imperative to creating meaningful conversations.

There are as many ways to listen as there are points of contact within your company. Companies form advisory groups, host analyst briefings, participate in special interest groups, all to create opportunities to converse with key stakeholders. It's not easy, and it requires that you invest significant time and resources. The results are worth it. Listening may be the single most effective way to sustain conversations with your key stakeholders.

Changing the Subject

Knowing when and how to change the subject of a conversation is crucial to sustaining interest. There are natural times to change the conversation, such as mergers, acquisitions, management changes, and new product or service introductions. Emotionally charged subjects must be handled with the utmost sensitivity to stakeholder concerns when changing the subject. Anything that smacks of misdirection will be met immediately with skepticism and scorn. Changing the subject should be used only when the company has legitimate news to discuss or when it's time to refresh the conversation.

New advertising and public relations programs are the ideal way to signal a change in direction. They can bring energy and interest to the new topic and provide a starting point for one-to-one conversations. But it's important to reach closure of one conversation before starting another.

Why Don't They Hang Up Delighted?

After the sale, the relationship building begins in earnest. Long-term success often depends on what is being measured. Here's an example: Customers calling a customer service center expect to be connected with an efficient, polite, well-trained service representative who handles their problem. The customer would be delighted to find someone who not only does all that, but who also provides empathy and makes a genuine personal connection.

The reason that customers rarely hang up delighted from a customer service call is that service centers are judged on efficiency and accuracy, not on building customer relationships. The centers aren't measured on, and therefore can't worry about, the fact that every customer contact is an opportunity to build and strengthen relationships through conversations. Taking the time to listen creates an authentic encounter that not only reinforces a customer's purchase decision but may lead to additional sales. The reduction in speed or volume of completed calls could easily be justified if it were measured against long-term customer satisfaction and additional purchases.

The End All

Lands' End call center representatives understand the importance of building relationships with the buyer. Callers to the Lands' End 800-number may be astounded at the level of service they encounter. Customer service representatives offer knowledgeable assistance in everything from finding the right snow gear for your climate to getting the right size pants for a growing child. They are relaxed and allow the caller to spend time on the phone, a strategy that may often result in additional sales, and certainly reinforces the company's reputation for quality.[3]

My Job Would Be Great If It Weren't for These Customers

Some companies struggle most with relationship building when the operating values become us-versus-them. In these organizations, the customer is looked upon as someone who doesn't get it, makes their job hard, or is a necessary evil. Customers who don't feel valued go away. All the warning signals are present; typically, conversations have turned into arguments and accusations. Collection agencies, airlines, car rentals, and software developers are all industries that struggle with customer service because so many of the calls are from distraught customers. Many times empathy is not part of the conversation. Even though senior managers would deny it, it's often their own drive for efficiency and lack of clear values that create this customer-toxic environment.

What to Do When the Conversation Breaks Down

Think of the last discussion you had, when out of frustration you said, "This isn't going anywhere." Conversations break down because we don't agree, the conversation has become irrelevant, or we've just lost interest.

For businesses, the greatest threat to breakdown is lack of agreement. The chasm that forms between a customer and the company can quickly grow into resentment and can ultimately destroy the relationship. Silence rarely mends a relationship. One-to-one communications are needed, pronto.

Great stories and lively conversations never make up for the fact that a company's products or services are no longer relevant to customers. People also lose interest in a conversation if they aren't being heard. Conversations can quickly be reinvigorated by focusing on the other party. In each case, being aware of the direction of a conversation and how it is going is crucial to keeping all stakeholders engaged.

Be Relentless

Creating and sustaining interesting conversations is hard work. Initiating the dialogue, keeping it fresh, and actively listening requires great energy. Conversations are harder than campaigns and messaging. There really is no beginning, middle, or end point to business conversations, because there is continuous building and sustaining of relationships.

You must be relentless in initiating and monitoring conversations. In advertising, that means keeping the creative work fresh. In public relations, it means continuously finding new and interesting ways to tell the company's story and to start conversations. In sales, it means regular contact and active listening to the customer. And in all parts of the company, it means finding time to hear, understand, and respond to stakeholders.

Engaging in a conversation is more challenging than redesigning the logo or creating a new corporate campaign. Few companies sustain the effort over the long haul. Those who do reap the rewards and continually align with customer values.

The Role of Advertising in Conversations

Advertising messages play a variety of roles in conversations. Advertising is perfect for initiating and sustaining conversations. It is also a very efficient way to change the subject of the conversation. With advertising, you can control message, control the environment in which the message appears, target a specific audience, and deliver the message at the most opportune time. It is because of the high level of control that advertising is so valuable in initiating conversations.

Advertising provides a perfect outlet to introduce your company, products, and conversations. By viewing the advertising message as the start of a conversation, it's easy to plan subsequent follow-up conversations through direct marketing, the Internet, and one-on-one conversations. All of these points of contact should be a continuation of the conversation started by advertising. Great advertising can get people to start talking about your brand. This can mark the beginning of some terrific conversations.

When used irresponsibly, advertising also has the potential of being a horrific waste of money and, worse, of damaging the company's brand reputation. We've all heard stories about ad agencies that are so focused on winning creative awards that their client's brand suffered. While there is some validity to those claims, most reputable agencies work very hard to build their client's business. The real danger comes from the areas described next.

Three Ways to Waste Your Advertising Budget

Money Waster Number 1: Lack of a Clear Strategy

Without a comprehensive understanding of the business, market, customer, and product, it's impossible to develop a strong strategic plan. A strong strategic plan is essential to doing great advertising. It's painfully obvious to customers, employees, and industry opinion leaders when the advertising message is superficial or trite. Conversations that begin with a superficial subject rarely evolve into anything meaningful.

A terrific creative idea cannot cover up a poor strategy, and poor strategy will not lead to a great customer relationship.

Because of this, a significant part of the value of building a strong rapport with your agency is that the team thoroughly understands your business and strategies. In the best of all worlds, this team is integral in helping you build market strategies and translate your strategies into compelling stories and conversations in the marketplace.

Money Waster Number 2: Creative by Committee

Most corporate cultures are built on consensus building. While this is a successful work process, it's a poor way to manage effective advertising. The problem is that in our advertising-saturated society we are all so familiar with the medium that many people believe they can do advertising. A group of executives would never consider taking a shot at engineering, legal contracts, or financial reports, but everybody is willing to tinker with the advertising. This usually results in a fuzzy, disjointed string of product or service claims, which typically are more important to the organization than relevant to customer. Advertising should be judged on how well it delivers the strategy and stays true to the brand. When everybody's talking, no one hears what's being said. Effective conversations can only take place with a clear and concise story.

Input for the advertising strategy should come from the marketing and business units. Don't fall prey to the syndrome noted by an advertising director of a Fortune 500 consumer goods company, who said, "We hire Picasso to do our advertising and then have forty-two people standing behind him telling him how to paint."

The creative approval process should be limited to one or two marketing professionals within the organization.

Money Waster Number 3: Lack of Consistency

One of the best ways to waste money is to starve an initiative. Without proper funding, it's impossible to reach the right target audience at a frequency that ensures your advertising message is received. Determining the right spending levels requires in-depth analysis of the market, audiences, and available advertising media. Clients often ask, "How many spots will I get for my ad budget?" That's not the right question. Instead of looking at media in terms of the number of spots or pages, think about how many target customers you are reaching, and how often.

It's not uncommon to see clients kill their marketing effort just at the moment that they were about to realize a real return on investment. Many companies view cutting advertising and marketing budgets as a painless way to reduce overall corporate spending, but they're wrong.

It's imperative that your message is in front of the customer at the moment they are planning or considering a purchase. The goal of consistent advertising is to ensure that your product is part of the conversation leading up to a purchase.

The Role of Public Relations in Conversations

Public relations (PR) is your most powerful tool for garnering and managing third party validation. Having others say positive things about your company, reputation, products, or services is imperative to gaining credibility in the marketplace. The role of public relations is to get others to join in your conversation.

The challenge, though, is that you have limited control of the message, since others decide when and where the message is placed.

Some conversations, such as independent user groups on the Internet, are completely out of your control. Public relations creates an opportunity to provide the most comprehensive, in-depth information on your company, product, or service. Unlike advertising, which is limited to a thirty-second TV commercial or single page print ad, PR gives your company the opportunity to get a three-minute news segment or feature article that provides the background and analysis necessary to tell your story.

Public relations is at the center of vital conversations, such as your CEO's 's interview with an influential journalist about a new initiative and its impact on your company's future. Public relations uses conversations to sustain important relationships.

The downside of public relations is that the story cuts both ways. You cannot always control what the media, analysts, or customers will say about your company. Like advertising, having a strong strategic plan is the basis for effective public relations. If you don't manage the process correctly, poor execution of the strategy can damage your corporate brand and reputation.

Three Ways PR Can Ruin Your Reputation

Reputation Killer Number 1: Lack of Access and Information

While public relations can help shape the conversation, it cannot control it. Many executives are tempted to fire the messenger, meaning the public relations firm, if their story doesn't go exactly as planned. A reporter's job is to dig up the truth. The job of public relations is to create and manage stakeholder relationships while clarifying a company's position on issues. Without access to senior management and a clear understanding of the facts, it is impossible for a public relations agency to effectively help you tell your side of the story. When there is a void in the story, the conversation usually turns to rumors and conjecture because people have a need to fill in the blanks. It is better to be part of the conversation than to be at the mercy of gossip.

Reputation Killer Number 2: Spinning Out of Control

The truth shall set you free. With the number of half-truths and denials heard from the business world these days, it seems that no one is very interested in truth. Instead, many companies misuse public relations to distort and spin stories. This may work in the short term, but the loss of credibility when the truth comes to light outweighs the initial advantage the company was trying to gain. Once trust is broken with the media, the reputation of the company, executives, and PR practitioners is difficult to restore. There is a fine balance between complete disclosure and the possible legal repercussions caused by that disclosure. This creates a tenuous relationship between corporate communications and legal departments. However, if your stakeholders cannot trust your word, you will be left out of the conversation. Maintaining a balance of credible and newsworthy information is always in the best interests of your company.

Reputation Killer Number 3: Wasting Opportunities

If your company insists on overreporting every insignificant corporate event, you may find you can't get proper coverage for really important news. It's like someone who talks and talks and talks but never really says anything. Eventually we all tune them out. Feature stories are few and far between, so don't waste them on issues that don't have a long-term impact for your company and its reputation.

Conversely, many companies never report their accomplishments or activities. Many times management feels threatened by the media and begins operating on the premise that no news is good news. These lost news opportunities often make the difference between being perceived as an industry leader or being perceived as a perennial contender. Leading the conversation creates opportunities to be known and admired.

Chapter Eight Summary

Balanced Conversation

Balanced Conversation requires bringing authentic intentions and wording, not stilted business speak, to customer interactions.

A real conversation requires common interests, discussion, listening, and a respect for one another's point of view.

Sales Versus Relationships

Creating meaningful conversations, centered on customer needs, is the best way to build relationships that result in long-term sales.

Creating a Conversation

Describing all advertising and public relations as "creative content" blurs the lines and expands the possibilities.

Stories

Every company has a story that is the center of all stakeholder conversations.

Core Narrative

The Core Narrative includes basic history, vision, characters, pinnacle events, side stories, and conclusion.

Stakeholder Points of Contact

Outlining all possible stakeholder points of contact defines how creative content can be used to create conversations.

Initiating a Conversation

Narratives that align with stakeholder values create compelling stories that are memorable and effective.

Sustaining a Conversation
Sustaining a conversation requires reciprocity, both talking and listening.

Keep the Message, Change the Inflection
The personalized conversation: Same topic + different group = new inflection.

Changing the Subject
Knowing when to change the subject sustains interest and keeps the conversation fresh.

When the Conversation Breaks Down
The loss of interest in the conversation occurs when parties disagree or one party doesn't feel heard.

Be Relentless
Creating conversations is more difficult than executing traditional advertising and PR campaigns. The payoff is more opportunities to build relationships with stakeholders.

Three Ways to Waste Your Advertising Budget

1. Lack of a clear strategy
2. Creative by committee
3. Lack of consistency

Three Ways PR Can Ruin Your Reputation

1. Lack of access and information
2. Spinning out of control
3. Wasting opportunities

Creating and Maintaining Balance

Assessment and Alignment

Alignment and Assessment

With practice, balance does not need
to be a high-wire act.

Deploying The BalancedBrand System with discipline will ensure that you are in alignment with your stakeholders. Management of your brand and reputation will become second nature to the whole organization because of the processes you have put in place. Everyone will understand their role in building and maintaining strong stakeholder relations.

The challenge still remains in implementing BalancedBrand throughout your organization. Each component of The Balanced-Brand System requires a high level of commitment. Because the vision for a BalancedBrand is far more encompassing than traditional marketing, it requires rethinking how your entire organization works together and goes to market. Here are some guidelines for smoothing the way to implementation and lasting success.

Why Stakeholder Alignment Matters

If corporate values aren't aligned with stakeholder values, you risk hurting or destroying crucial stakeholder relationships. Ignorance of those values is no excuse for acting contrary to stakeholder standards. Nike was caught off guard and therefore could not explain its use of sweatshop subcontractors, which resulted in severe customer and reputation backlash.

Stakeholders expect companies to understand and abide by their personal values. Getting your organization into alignment with those values is crucial. Of course you can't perfectly align all stakeholder values with corporate values, so your job is to prioritize each stakeholder group and determine which values are essential for alignment. This exercise provides a clear picture of your position with the stakeholders. With this information, you can build contingency plans based on your company's current and future actions while anticipating stakeholder reactions.

Finding the Right Partners

As Jim Collins stated in his book *Good to Great*,[1] getting the right people on board is the first step. This is also true for inside and outside partners. The agencies you use to do your advertising and public relations must be willing to collaborate to achieve a BalancedBrand.

The idea of stakeholder alignment and starting conversations may be seen as threatening by some partners, because agencies may have never before worked within this framework. From an agency perspective, BalancedBrand cannot be about budgets or turf wars, but must be relentless in initiating and sustaining relationship-building conversations. This requires new ways of thinking about traditional communications approaches.

Those agencies willing to adapt conversation-based marketing will find that they are doing better and more results-oriented work for their clients. BalancedBrand helps create exciting, fresh creative work for all partners.

The marketplace is changing, competition is getting stronger, and the business environment has never been more demanding. It's time for new, innovative thinking. Your outside agencies and consultants need a place at the table as strategic partners helping to lead the change. Agencies that are unwilling or unable to work at this level may be detrimental to your overall efforts.

Implementation Timelines

As soon as your organization has committed to putting the budget and resources behind BalancedBrand, the next question is how long it will take. If your organization has the necessary levels of commitment, time, and budget, The BalancedBrand System can be in place eight to eighteen months after its inception. Here are some suggested timelines for each stage.

TIMELINE
to completion

brandassessment

6 weeks to 4 months

stakeholderassessment

6 weeks to 4 months
benchmark quarterly or biannually

balancedculture

3 to 6 months

balancedconversation

3 to 6 months   8 to 12 months
to design   *to implement*

Brand Assessment   This work can be completed in six weeks to three months, depending on implementation team schedules. In many organizations, a significant amount of work has already been accomplished in the areas of corporate values, reputation, brand personality, positioning, and brand messaging. The goal of Brand Assessment is not to reinvent the wheel, but rather to identify a solid base from which your company can compare its values, brand, and reputation with the values and perceptions of your stakeholders.

Stakeholder Assessment   The initial research and analysis necessary to complete Values Mapping of your stakeholders will take approximately six weeks for qualitative research to four months for quantitative research, depending on the size and logistics of recruiting and surveying the targeted stakeholder groups. This work can be conducted simultaneously with Brand Assessment initiatives. We recommend benchmarking stakeholder values and employee engagement annually.

A good values monitoring program will quickly identify potential shifts in values. Major social, industry, and economic events also trigger times when your company should monitor shifts in stakeholder values.

Balanced Culture   Changing corporate culture is an iterative process, starting with clearly articulating the vision and rationale for the change. Once employees understand how this new vision affects their jobs and careers, they can begin to give the feedback and buy-in necessary for authentic culture change.

Most organizations use outside consulting firms in developing employee programs through human resources, training, and employee communications. Balanced Culture takes approximately three months to design and eight to twelve months to implement. Even with this longer time frame, it's important to keep in mind that Balanced Culture will be the catalyst for ensuring your company is in true alignment with stakeholder values.

Balanced Conversation   Initiating conversations takes approximately the same amount of time as building and launching a new advertising or public relations program. The only extra step is getting your outside agencies on board as part of the strategic process prior to developing new communications initiatives.

Typically, the lead time for these activities is three to six months. Keep in mind that additional communications will be necessary to explain the company's new direction to all stakeholders. You'll also be developing a Manifesto for Change and a Unifying Customer Experience book. All these elements can be coordinated and developed using internal and external communications resources as a single, cohesive BalancedBrand team. This integration is based on the overall strategic intent of moving the organization and its marketing initiatives in a new direction.

Global Balance

Using the basic BalancedBrand tenets, it is possible and advantageous to apply this philosophy on a global basis. The incorporation of cultural values as they impact stakeholder values represents a significant challenge for all global businesses. Nations, as well as businesses, are affected by the forces identified. Understanding local cultural values can provide a roadmap for greater harmony and cooperation worldwide. BalancedBrand ensures that you can offer a unified customer experience based on values of alignment throughout the world. It is a perfect antidote in combating growing anti-American sentiments. For multinational companies, BalancedBrand is a powerful and indispensable business tool.

Losing the Globalization Debate

In a recent speech to the U.S. Chamber of Commerce, Mike Eskew, CEO of UPS, outlined five areas that business leaders needed to address in order to restore the bruised reputation of global trade. Those areas are defined as:

1. *Education:* Eskew stated that we have to ask ourselves, "Are we producing enough engineers, scientists, technologists, material researchers, manufacturing and trade specialists, and other

professional services that are in such huge demand and so needed to ensure our competitive vitality?" The answer is, of course, a resounding "No." Nearly fifty years ago, *Sputnik* not only launched the race for space but was a catalyst for encouraging tens of thousands of American kids to study science, math, and engineering. We need a similar wake-up call today.

2. *Global Trade Literacy:* We should encourage organizations such as Southern Center for International Studies, which has developed a curriculum to train every social studies teacher in the state of Georgia on global trade and geography.

3. *The Anti-Globalization Movement:* We can support programs and policies that address training and career development for all those who have been displaced by international trade.

4. *Innovation:* Twenty-five years ago people were afraid the United States was going to lose its jobs to Japan. Even greater numbers were worried about having their careers rendered obsolete by technology. That mirrors the fears we see today, only the names have changed. Instead of Japan, it's India and China. Instead of technology, it's globalization. American business did what we historically have done best—we innovate. Tom Peters reminds us that in the process of innovating, we replaced 44 million antiquated jobs with 73 million new jobs. The bulk of those jobs required knowledge of technology. The net effect was 29 million new, higher-paying, higher-skilled jobs between 1980 and 1998. We need to continue our rich tradition of innovation.

5. *Foreign Affairs:* Corporate diplomacy is as important as political diplomacy. Anti-Americanism abroad is a significant concern. We've seen a serious slide in American business's favorability around the world, and in a short time frame.[2]

Eskew's insights are extremely helpful in framing the critical issues surrounding global trade.

Is Your Future in Balance?

Creating and maintaining a BalancedBrand is the key to creating an authentic competitive advantage through relationship building. Aligning values and starting conversations has long been the road to building trust and relationships. Corporate brands and reputations are the natural extension of interpersonal relationships. By finding common ground and shared values, everyone wins.

Chapter Nine Summary

Why Stakeholder Alignment Matters

Stakeholders expect companies to understand and abide by their values, so accurately and continuously measuring stakeholder values is critical to building a strong brand and a strong reputation.

Changing Culture

If you don't have senior management and employee buy-in, you won't have the internal cultural change necessary to create a BalancedBrand.

Finding the Right Partners

Your partners and agencies need to embrace The Balanced-Brand System or move on.

Timelines

Give it time to work. Timeframes for completion range from eight to eighteen months.

Global Balance

The tenets of BalancedBrand when applied to international business can create a global advantage.

Notes

Chapter One

1. Ronald J. Alsop, *The 18 Immutable Laws of Corporate Reputation: Creating, Protecting, and Repairing Your Most Valuable Asset.* New York: Free Press, 2004.
2. "Wal-Mart's CEO on Offensive Against Critics," Associated Press, January 13, 2005.
3. Justin Wolfers, "The Business of Sports: An Introduction to Sports Economics." Presentation to the Young President's Organization on February 6, 2003. Available at:http://bpp.wharton.upenn.edu/jwolfers/Papers/Comments/The%20Business%20of%20Sports.pdf
4. "Tiffany Open Letter to Forest Service Chief Dale Bosworth," *Washington Post*, March 23, 2004.
5. Becky Kramer and Karen Dorn Steel, "Jeweler Says Wilderness Worth More Than Mine," *The Spokesman-Review*, March 25, 2004, p. A1.
6. Jewelers of America Association, News Release, September 16, 2004.
7. Richard Heller, *Forbes Magazine*, November 11, 2002, p. 170.
8. Leonard L. Berry, "The Collaborative Organization: Leadership Lessons from Mayo Clinic," *Organizational Dynamics*, Vol. 33, No. 3(2004), pp. 228–242.
9. Ibid.
10. Mayo Clinic, Patient Brand Monitor, 2003.

Chapter Two

1. Don E. Schultz and Heidi F. Schultz, *"Three Pathways to Measuring and Evaluating Brands,"* Kellogg on Branding: The Marketing Faculty of The Kellogg School of Management. Hoboken, N.J.: John Wiley & Sons, 2005.
2. Background information and quotes from Charles Fombrun, July 18, 2005.
3. Gordon Slovut, "Salmonella Traced to Schwan's Ice Cream," *Minneapolis Star-Tribune*, October 8, 1994.
4. Timothy Sellnow and Mort Sarabakhsh, "Practical Communication Guidelines for Effective Crisis Management," *FIU Hospitality Review*, Spring 1999, p. 38.

Chapter Four

1. Mike Moser, *United We Brand: How to Create a Cohesive Brand That's Seen, Heard, and Remembered.* Boston: Harvard Business School Press, 2003.
2. David A. Aaker, *Building Strong Brands.* New York: Free Press, 1996.

Chapter Five

1. Bill George, *Authentic Leadership: Rediscovering the Secrets to Creating Lasting Value.* San Francisco: Jossey-Bass, 2003.
2. Allyce Bess, "Trading Up: The New Pursuit of Happiness," *St. Louis Post-Dispatch*, April 4, 2004.
3. James Twitchell, *Living It Up: America's Love Affair with Luxury.* New York: Simon & Schuster, 2003.
4. Richard A. Easterlin, "Explaining Happiness," *Proceedings of the National Academy of Sciences (PNAS)*, September 16, 2003, Volume 100, number 19.

5. Kay Miller, "If Money Makes You Rich, How Much Would Make You Happy?" *Minneapolis Star Tribune*, December 9, 2003, p.1E.

6. B. J. Bullert, *Strategic and Public Relations' Sweatshops and the Making of a Global Movement* (#2000–14). Cambridge, Mass.: President and Fellows of Harvard College, 2000.

7. Diana Farrell, McKinsey Global Institute, "Jobs Onshore and Off-shore." Presentation to World Economic Forum, 2004. Available at: http://www.mckinsey.com/ideas/wef2004/takingpulse/offshoring.asp

8. "IBM to Cut 13,000 jobs," Reuters, May 4, 2005.

9. Chris Wille, "Conserving Coffee Lands and Livelihoods," *The Canopy*, Fall 2003. Available at Rainforest-Alliance.edu Rainforest Alliance, 2003.

10. Geoff Calkins, Community Level Investment Sources, "We've Taken the Greed out of Sports," *Fast Company*, November 2000, p. 170.

11. "Bayport: 100 Year Anniversary," January 21, 2003. Available at Andersenwindows.com

Chapter Seven

1. Background information from Jim Haymaker at Cargill. Personal communication, May 28, 2005.

2. Howard Gardner, *Changing Minds: The Art and Science of Changing Our Own and Other People's Minds*. Boston: Harvard Business School Press, 2004.

3. Manifesto, March 26, 2004, courtesy of Lawson, May 30, 2005.

4. Josuha Cooper Ramo, "Winner Take All," *Time*, September 16, 1996.

5. Paul Andrews, *How the Web Was Won*. New York: Broadway Books, 1999.

6. Manifesto in Action, published September 1, 2004, courtesy of Lawson, May 30, 2005.

7. Reputation Institute, RepTrack, New York, August 2004.

Chapter Eight

1. Fara Warner, "What to Expect When You're Expecting a Mini-Cooper," *New York Times*, January 25, 2004.
2. Lawson Core Narrative, June 8, 2005, courtesy of Lawson.
3. Lorrie Grant, "Lands' End Is an Ultimate Online Model," *USA Today*, December 12, 2004.

Chapter Nine

1. James C. Collins, *Good to Great: Why Some Companies Make the Leap—And Others Don't*. New York: HarperBusiness, 2001.
2. Michael L. Eskew, U.S. Chamber of Commerce. Speech at CEO Leadership Series Luncheon. Washington, D.C., September 29, 2004. Adapted for *Chief Executive*, April 2005, p. 14.

Glossary

BalancedBrand The continuous assessment and alignment of corporate values with key stakeholder values.

The BalancedBrand System A comprehensive process that assesses and aligns corporate values with key stakeholder values. The BalancedBrand System processes are Brand Assessment, Stakeholder Assessment, Balanced Culture, and Balanced Conversation.

Balanced Conversation The use of advertising, public relations, and nontraditional communications to create ongoing dialogue between companies and their stakeholders.

Balanced Culture The internal adjustments made by companies to align their corporate values with stakeholder values.

Balanced Value Pyramid Tool for determining value of product of service. The three dimensions of the Balanced Pyramid are 1) Aspiration (How well does the company's product or service satisfy a purchaser's needs and desires?); 2) Process (Does the product manufacturing process or service delivery reflect the expected standard levels set by all stakeholders?); and 3) Impact (How does the product or service positively or negatively affect the community or the environment?).

Brand A set of promises, associations, images, and emotions that companies create to build loyalty with their customers.

Brand Assessment A comprehensive overview of an organization's vision, operating values, reputation, brand message, brand personality, and position.

Brand Personality The age, origin, size, and character of a company.

Brand Strength A method of evaluating a brand by measuring its financial strength, stakeholder support, and overall brand awareness.

Builders A stakeholder group that includes boards of directors, employees, distributors, dealers, and any other group that works to build, distribute, or sell a company's product or service.

Buyers A stakeholder group that includes anyone who directly purchases or influences the purchase of a company's product or service.

Content Delivery The placement of paid media as well as the exploration of finding new and novel ways to create conversations and all points of contact with the stakeholder.

Content Development The development of all communications surrounding a stakeholder conversation, including advertising, public relations, direct marketing, promotion, sales support, and events.

Core Narrative The most relevant story about a company. The Core Narrative includes history, vision, characters, pinnacle events, side stories, and conclusion. The Core Narrative is the source for all other stakeholder communications.

Crisis Management A communications and organizational plan designed to help companies effectively deal with a major problem or disaster.

Dominant Values A set of personal or professional values that evoke strong positive or negative feelings resulting in direct action with a company, brand, reputation, product, and service.

Flashpoint Moment when a shift in stakeholder values reaches a threshold that causes a positive or negative reaction to a company, product, service, brand, or reputation.

Funders A stakeholder group that includes investors, analysts, foundations, and private owners of a company or nonprofit organization.

Influencers A stakeholder group that includes community, media, industry leaders, opinion leaders, special interest groups, industry watchdogs, and government, all of which can change an organization's brand and reputation.

Latent Values A set of personal or professional principles that a stakeholder has assigned to a company, brand, product, or service but does not feel strongly enough to act on.

Manifesto A public declaration of intent by a company as to how it's going to conduct business to create alignment with its stakeholders.

1,000-Day Plan Method that incorporates long-term plan broken into ten 100-day increments. Using the 100-day increments helps the internal organization focus on short-term goals to achieve long-term strategies.

Operating Values A set of informal corporate values that are inherent to the culture and are used by employees and managers to operate the business and interact with stakeholders.

Positioning The process of mental sorting people go through as they try to define, differentiate, and evaluate companies, products, and services.

Qualitative Research One-to-one or focus group research designed to gather in-depth attitudes, perceptions, or reactions on the subject. This feedback is not statistically measurable because of the small sample size.

Quantitative Research Research conducted with a large enough respondent sample size to be statistically measurable.

RepTrack A standardized research tool that measures reputation strength. RepTrack is conducted by the Reputation Institute.

Reputation Overall perceptions of company, brand, product, or service held by outside stakeholders.

Stakeholder Anyone who influences or has a vested interest in a company.

Stakeholder Agenda A unique set of personal or professional values held by a stakeholder group. Each stakeholder group's values may be in conflict with other stakeholder groups or a company, brand, product, or service.

Stakeholder Alignment Actions taken by an organization that are meant to create alignment with stakeholder values.

Stakeholder Assessment The assessment of key stakeholders' personal and professional values that are used to judge a company's products, services, brand, and reputation.

Stakeholder Points of Contact All possible interactions between a company and a stakeholder. Stakeholder points of contact identify the opportunities to initiate or sustain a conversation.

Stakeholder Values Map Tool that measures the intensity of the personal or professional values each stakeholder group holds in the areas of Aspiration, Process, and Impact.

Stated Values Formal corporate values found in annual reports or corporate literature. These values may or may not be actually held by the company's employees.

Third Party Validation Outside sources that provide analysis, comment, and opinion on a company's brand, reputation, products, and services. These sources include customers, shareholders, analysts, opinion leaders, industry experts, and the media.

3R Brand Equation Formula that examines each stakeholder value based on relevance and relationship to determine the ROI.

Unifying Customer Experience A booklet or brochure that describes, from the customer's point of view, what the ideal product or service would look like in 1,000 days. This document would be used to help employees of an organization identify what actions need to be taken to satisfy the customer's future wants and needs.

Values A set of personal or professional standards that guide behavior.

Values Monitoring The continuous evaluation of stakeholder values used in calibrating corporate actions.

Vision Outlines the nature of a business and identifies the organization's future aspirations and goals.

Acknowledgments

Writing a book is a humbling experience. Without the generous help of many people, *Balanced Brand* would still be a loose set of ideas. I would like to begin by thanking Julie Kendrick, my writing partner and editor. Julie did a wonderful job helping to shape the ideas and writing a cogent book. Julie organized materials, conducted additional research, and corrected a multitude of errors.

As the concept of *Balanced Brand* was taking shape, I had the good fortune of being introduced to Scott Meyer. Scott has one of the most fertile and brilliant marketing minds I've ever met. He played a pivotal role in helping to create and test the concepts of The BalancedBrand System at Lawson.

Kathleen Bridget Clark was by far my biggest supporter, confidante, and ghostwriter. She spent an enormous amount of time fretting over and fixing my writing. Without a doubt, Kathy made this book much more interesting and readable.

I would also like to thank Jeri Quest for playing mental Ping-Pong to help sort out and test assessment concepts. Jeri was willing to carefully translate my sketchy values assessment thoughts into workable models.

Don Schultz is one the most innovative brand experts working in the field today. His insights and time generously spent critiquing The BalancedBrand System were invaluable. Don's global perspective elevated the thinking and direction of this book.

Charles Fombrun was kind enough to introduce me to some of the world's reputation thought leaders at the Reputation Institute. The work of the Reputation Institute is setting the standard for global corporate governance.

Jim Haymaker opened the door to Cargill's journey, which provided a glimpse of how a world-class company uses values and employee engagement to change direction. Through Jim's strategic work at Cargill, I was able to validate the importance of values in driving business outcomes.

I'm indebted to Dr. Patricia Simmons, Carleton Rider, John La Forgia, Amy Davis, and Dr. Leonard Berry for providing insights and counsel to tell the Mayo Clinic story.

At the completion of the first draft, I asked for help from business executives Gary Johnson, Rob Longendyke, Janet Sterk, Chris Causey, Toni Louw, and Ellen Breyer to review and challenge every aspect of *Balanced Brand*. Without their critique, questions, and input, I would never have seen this book through the eyes of outside experts. Needless to say, the book went through a total rewrite.

The challenge of successfully bringing *Balanced Brand* to market was given to Dave Mona, David Stillman, Chris Mahai, Chris Causey, Scott Meyer, Jeri Quest, Dan Buettner, and Mary Jeffries. Their experience and ideas ensure that *Balanced Brand* will reach the people who can change the course of business.

Balanced Brand would be an unfinished, unpublished manuscript if it weren't for the efforts of Paul Mahon, publishing attorney extraordinaire, and Jim Levine at LevineGreenberg Literary Agency, whose thoughtful guidance helped the manuscript find its way to Susan Williams, Executive Editor at Jossey-Bass. I can't thank Susan enough for believing in the power of values and for how quickly she turned this project into a viable business book. A special thanks to Rob Brandt, Assistant Editor; Mary Garrett, Senior Production Editor; Caroline Carlstroem, Marketing Manager; and the rest of the Jossey-Bass team who are committed to ensuring that every aspect of this book was done right. Their professionalism is evident on every page.

The real unsung heroes of this concept are my friends and colleagues at The Foley Group. Kim Thelen, Laura Shiue, Johnny Mackin, Juliee Oden, Ruth Edstrom, Lori Leibig, Kim Lokken, and the rest of the agency have survived multiple iterations of this project. Not only has BalancedBrand challenged the way we think about marketing but it's changed the way we do our jobs. Without your support, bringing this idea to fruition would have been impossible.

What would be a proper acknowledgment without thanking your mother? Anne, you are the best. Sorry I haven't called.

Last and certainly not least, to my family, Cindy, Maureen, and David, who have cheerfully provided the support, love, and encouragement to let me chase this dream. My wife, Cindy, is an extraordinary writer with a brilliant mind. Her willingness to share her talent through endless rewrites is a tribute to her generosity and love. Maureen, you may be disappointed that you weren't mentioned first in the book, but you and David are first in my heart.

About the Authors

John Foley is the founder of the brand agency The Foley Group. His agency has been providing strategic brand planning, advertising, and public relations since 1986 for organizations including Ameriprise Financial, Cargill, Caterpillar, Coca-Cola USA, Hazelden, Lawson, 3M, Tiffany & Co., United Healthcare, and the University of Minnesota.

In addition, he is Chief Executive Officer of BALANCED-BRAND LLC, which provides values-based brand and reputation consultation in the United States and the United Kingdom. Foley is currently on the boards of the Carlson Brand Enterprise at the University of Minnesota, the Minnesota chapter of American Association of Advertising Agencies, the Design Institute, and the Reputation Institute.

Julie Kendrick is a business writer with expertise in the area of motivation and performance improvement. Her client list includes Fortune 100 companies in the areas of automotive manufacturing, pharmaceutical and medical device manufacturing, and telecommunications.

Index

J

Japan, competition from, 160
Java, 118
Jernigan, D., 82, 83
Jewelers of America, 13
Johnson & Johnson, 24, 26

K

Keller, K. L., 21
Kmart, 10
Kowalski, M., 12–13

L

Labor practices: influence of, on reputa-
tion, 6–8, 155; Latent Values and, 93;
process values and, 74–78
Lands' End, 142
Language: influence of, 129; traditional
business, 129, 130–131
Latent Values, 91, 92, 97, 169
Lawson Software: Core Narrative of,
136–137; initial public offering (IPO)
of, 113–114; Intentia merger of,
114–116, 136–137; Manifesto in Action
of, 120–122; Manifesto of, 115–116, 137
Leadership: compelling narratives from,
111; perception of, 24
Lifetime ownership, 80–81
Lincoln, A., 11
Listening, 138, 140, 141–142
Literacy, global trade, 160
Local governments, impact values and, 80
L'Oreal, 24, 26

M

Major League Baseball (MLB), 9, 10
Malfeasance, public intolerance for,
40–41. See also Scandals
Manifesto for Change, 111–116, 125,
159, 169
Manifesto in Action (Lawson Software),
120–122
Marketing: Balanced Conversation
and, 42–43, 129–151; brand and reputation in, 3; campaign-based versus
conversation-based, 132; positioning
and, 57–58; 20% rule and, 72; weak,
32–33

Marketing departments, aspiration values
and, 84
Mayo, C., 14
Mayo, W., 14
Mayo Clinic, 13–16
Mayo Model of Service, 15
May's School of Business, 15
McDonald's, 24, 69
McKinsey & Co., 72, 77
McKinsey Global Institute, 77
Measurement: of brand strength, 21–23,
34; of reputation, 23–26, 34; of stake-
holder return on investment, 89–98,
94, 95, 97; of values strength, 91–94
Media relations, 26, 28, 40, 41; Balanced
Conversation approach to, 133,
147–149
Medtronic, 65
Memphis Redbirds, 82–83
Memphis Redbirds Baseball Foundation,
82–83
Mental short lists, 57, 60
Messaging, 134, 138, 140
Methodology, 94–96, 97
Microsoft, 24, 26, 117–118
Midwesterners, preconceptions about, 56
Milestones, 122, 126
MINI Cooper, 132–133
Mission-driven organizations, 65
Mistakes, handling, 29–30
Monitoring system, 94–96, 98, 123–124,
158, 171
Moser, M., 51
Motion, balance in, 123–124, 126

N

Narratives: Core, 133–137, 150, 168; ele-
ments of, 135–136; Lawson Software
example of, 136–137; in Manifesto for
Change, 111, 112; power of, 133–134;
in Unifying Customer Experience, 119
National Basketball Association (NBA),
9, 10
National Football League (NFL), 9, 10
National Hockey League (NHL), 9–10
Net present value, 21
Netscape, 118
Nike, 77, 155
Northwestern University, 21
Nurses, turnover rates of, 15–16